PROFIT THROUGH QUALITY

Profit through Quality

Management control of Q and R activities

SIDNEY WEINBERG

Foreword by

The Rt Hon Lord Robens of Woldingham

Gower Press

First published in Great Britain by Gower Press Limited
13 Bloomsbury Square, London WC1
1969

To my daughter Hilary

Set in 10 on 12 point Plantin and printed by
Hazell Watson & Viney Ltd, Aylesbury,
Bucks

Contents

FOREWORD *by Lord Robens*   x

INTRODUCTION   xi
  Structure of the book—Acknowledgements

1 PROFIT IN QUALITY AND RELIABILITY   1
   Meaning of quality—Meaning of reliability—Economic
   rewards of Q and R activities

2 BASIC REQUIREMENTS OF A Q AND R POLICY   12
   Ascertaining requirements of customer or user—
   Embodiment of requirements in design—Specifying—
   Proving the specification—Manufacturer's acceptance of
   responsibility for compliance with requirements—
   Inspection—Advice to customer—Feed of information
   from operations to manufacturer—Organisation for overall
   control of quality

3 HUMAN CONTRIBUTION TO QUALITY   26
   Company objectives and the background to Q and R
   activities—Middle management responsibility—Shop floor
   management—Physical characteristics of people—
   Industrial motivations—Automation—Workers and
   standards

4 INCREASING THE PROPORTION OF GOOD QUALITY   43
   Product examination—Monitoring performance—
   Isolation and elimination of defects

CONTENTS

5 STANDARDISATION AND SPECIFICATION   58

Implication of the two words—Standards organisations—
Specification—NCQR/BSI *Guide to the Preparations of
Specifications*—Standardisation practice—Special effects of
standardisation in large organisations—Means of achieving
standardisation—Procedures in the case of departures from
specification by user and manufacturer—Reasons for not
standardising

6 ROLE OF INSPECTION IN ENSURING QUALITY   77

Factory inspection—Inspection by the user

7 DEVELOPMENT I: IMPROVEMENT AND INNOVATION   94

Development for improvement—Development for
innovation—Development policy as it affects and is affected
by middle management—Development by means of
standardisation—Types of testing—Specification test
equipment

8 DEVELOPMENT II: INCREASE IN RELIABILITY   115

Statistical view of reliability as a probability—Measurement
of reliability—Reliability of systems—Important elements
in a complex system—Stand-by design—Reliability of
"one-off" equipment—Use of operational data to increase
reliability—Principle factors which affect reliability—
Direct causes of unreliability

9 PURCHASE OF QUALITY   133

How to choose from a range of qualities—Price per unit of
quality—Purchasing to specification—Methods of purchase
not geared to lowest first cost—Possible effect of
arrangements for budgetary control—The magnitude and
effect of "cost of ownership"—Approval of manufacturer
by vendor rating—Requirement for QC systems—
Approval of product—Technical considerations for
purchasing—Cost of too high levels of quality and
reliability—Purchasing in cases of failure of quality

CONTENTS

APPENDICES

1 TYPICAL COMPLAINTS CODE   153

Delivery—Quality—Customer orientation—Miscellaneous
complaints

2 GUIDE TO THE PREPARATION OF SPECIFICATIONS   155

Comprehensive list of items which may be required in a
specification

INDEX   165

Illustrations

1 Quality improvement in action   10

2 Organisation for control of quality: product based   22

3 Return on investment in operator training   32

4 Proportion of unavoidable waste   48

5 Profit performance   51

6 Vital few defects   56

7 Simplified quality control chart   81

8 Control chart for minimum value   82

9 Development by means of standardisation   99

10 Effect of the reliability of components on the reliability of an assembly   119

11 Cost of quality   135

12 Price behaviour in relation to quality   136

Foreword

by Lord Robens of Woldingham, PC, DCL, LLD

There is no doubt that if British industry is to compete successfully in the markets of the world, attention needs to be focused particularly on the subjects of quality and reliability. The recent Quality and Reliability Year, 1966–7, drew much-needed attention to this often overlooked field; the present work follows on from this, drawing upon the author's wide experience of the subject.

This admirable book, written for the general manager rather than the narrowly technical, identifies the importance of these key areas and suggests many modes of attack on the problem. The author stresses, and quite rightly, the critical responsibility that top management bears for quality and reliability; his detailed studies suggest many far-reaching conclusions for all sectors of industry. The important point is that control and emphasis on quality and reliability are essential prerequisites for successful commercial management. Concern with quality and reliability must become part of the basis of managerial practice; this book explains how, by the application of a few simple concepts and techniques, enormous benefits can accrue.

The author has a real contribution to make in a field of great potential value to British industry and I would certainly commend this book to all managers, whatever their size of undertaking, whose concern is with increasing profitability, better customer relations and more successful design and performance.

Introduction

The object of this book is to emphasise the economic significance of quality and reliability activities.

This cannot be done by clouding the arguments with disciplines and techniques. Those who attempt to convey the ideas should therefore be production managers or, better still, management accountants rather than Q and R specialists. Instead of merely promoting such specialised subjects as Statistical Quality Control, the control of quality must be presented as a necessary step to profit increase. Publications in this field, however, appear to be written largely by specialists for other specialists. They therefore tend to generate refinements in techniques rather than seize the imagination of management. The preachers have been talking mainly to the converted.

Management cannot be convinced merely by exposure to refined details, however important, in the whole of quality and reliability activities. Those details would play little part in any preliminary investigations leading to a choice of policy and subsequent organisational moves.

The simple test of successful management is that of profitability. Few, if any, activities are justified unless they increase profit. All measures taken—to improve safety, reduce health hazards, ameliorate working conditions, provide social perquisities, increase interest and also pleasure and pride in work, increase pay—result in greater productivity. This is true even when, or especially when, they are taken from the highest humanitarian motives.

An organisation which is imbued with the feeling that the individual's interests are the concern of the management is on the way to success. The social scientists have long recognised the enormous effects of "morale" on the performance of factories. Nothing increases morale more than involvement, which is the first requirement for Q and R.

The terms of reference for chief executives can be stated in very simple terms, such as: ". . . to make a profit this year, a larger one next year, and a still larger one the year after." This says nothing about Q and R, or even about production or costs. The methods by which the requisite state of affairs is achieved are left to them to choose, by policy and planning. Procedures proposed can, therefore, only get a hearing if they can be justified by profitability—if not now, later.

This has not been done. What was said was that Q and R was a good thing, a noble thing, a virtue. Injunctions to introduce Q and R were in the same category as injunctions not to sin. The high priests of SQC and other techniques (all of the utmost value and importance in their place) expected them to be accepted for their own sake. What it is hoped to convey here is that Q and R activities must be examined for potentiality to increase profit and that all other means to do so, *without exception*, achieve best results when operated compatibly with Q and R procedures.

The National Productivity Year held in Great Britain in 1963, led naturally to this latter conclusion, and so to the Quality and Reliability Year, 1966–7. Profitability was the theme of the latter, and Q and R activities were discussed on this basis and not by techniques. Management, which, almost for the first time in this field, was present in force, received the assurance of the objectives that were directly related to the balance sheet and the benefits that would accrue to all.

Case studies have been prepared under three headings of which the first concerned itself with the manufacturing industries. Generalisations of the requirements were extracted from these and are dealt with in Chapter 2 so that one industry might benefit from the practices and experiences in another. Technical methods were hardly dwelt upon. It was shown that the requirement for these would follow when the correct attitudes and atmosphere had been established and that they were the tools for the jobs prescribed.

It is believed, and there has since been presented some quantified evidence in support, that QRY had a considerable impact on many sectors of British industry. The symptoms of this were the subsequent increasing numbers of advertisements for Quality Managers, and so on; the raising of quality and reliability points in discussions not necessarily devoted to these subjects; and the requests for, and good attendance at, conferences, symposia, and courses on these matters designed for management levels.

The inspiration for this book came largely from the QR Year and the opportunities I had in meeting top executives and in discussing their problems. The conviction developed that there was a need for simple explanations of the meaning and significance of Q and R without becoming unduly involved in techniques. If experts in any one field pick it up they will undoubtedly find that it lacks "sophistication." In so far as techniques are mentioned at all, the aim is to provide for management a working knowledge of their principles; to "get with it." They will then find that it can all be classified under straight thinking. Some procedures, such as profit monitoring, are therefore approached from the aspect of production rather than accounting, which is a familiar and possibly more complex technique.

Although specific parts are devoted to the control of quality, this is what the whole book is about, for the subject is much more all-embracing than usually thought. Reference is generally to manufacture and products, by far the most common field of interest. Nevertheless, many of the principles of the control of quality are equally important in the provision of services. Large organisations have been dealt with in greater detail than small ones for the simple reason that in the former there are usually more complications of function; the user, for example, not being the actual purchaser. What can be achieved in a large organisation, however, can often be achieved in a small one if necessary condensations are made. It has also been necessary to jump from the manufacturer's viewpoint to that of the customer, and in many cases they are represented by the terms supplier on the one hand and purchaser or user on the other. It is hoped that the context makes the term unambiguous in each case.

Finally, the number of references to further reading have been restricted deliberately. Anyone who wishes to amplify one or other subject can easily obtain a considerable amount of published matter and advice from the British Productivity Council or the National Council for Quality and Reliability. The intention, however, was to paint an overall and fairly complete picture of attitudes and activities, and it is hoped that this has been achieved.

Structure of the book

Broadly speaking the book is divided into six parts. These are:

Chapters 1 and 2. The first two chapters give the starting point by providing definitions, showing the high potential rewards and describing the overall procedural requirements and organisation within which to operate Q and R activities.

Chapters 3 and 4. These chapters deal with the attitudes and relationships of the people concerned, at all levels, and then the methods that are used as normal adjuncts to production.

Chapter 5. Deals with standardisation as the platform on which the control of quality is erected.

Chapter 6. In this, the checking role of inspection is described from both the supplier's and the user's points of view. This is the stage where compliance with the requirements is demonstrated to the customer.

Chapters 7 and 8. Development procedures, largely by testing, are first discussed. Increase in reliability and its special techniques is the other aspect of development.

Chapter 9. This provides a view of some of the problems of the purchaser of quality. These can have over-riding influences on the supplier's arrangements previously described.

Acknowledgements

I want to acknowledge permission received from the National Coal Board, the Association of Mining Electrical and Mechanical Engineers, the Institution of Production Engineers, and the British Standards Institution, to reproduce some material which I prepared for their various publications. I also want to thank my colleagues in the National Council for Quality and Reliability and in the British Productivity Council for valuable discussions which have helped to formulate my ideas. Lastly, I express my gratitude to the Institution of Mechanical Engineers, whose representative I am on the NCQR and which enables me to involve myself in this subject of national importance.

S Weinberg

One

Profit in Quality and Reliability

The words "Quality and Reliability" are now bandied about as if they were a single hyphenated word. However, although interdependent, they are not one and the same thing, and before going further it is necessary to identify them.

Meaning of quality

Everyone knows the meaning of quality. It is probably true to say that if asked for definitions, many of these would be roughly the same, indicating some sort of aura surrounding an article or a service. Quality was—and it is hoped still is—implicit in a stamp (for example, "British Made") but sometimes it was assumed to be merely a function of price. With the advent of formal procedures in the control of quality, it became necessary to know *what* was to be controlled; more rational definitions were sought and attempts were made to quantify quality. Everyone concerned has his own definition and, in many cases, there arise controversies as to which definition is correct. Not least do these discussions take place in the supposedly knowledgeable professional circles in which "quality" may appear in the title of a particular organisation.

The definition of quality given here is that of the writer's own opinion. It is not incompatible with others and, in so far as the definition may be used in the control of quality, the end results in terms of achievement can be identical.

Quality, simply, is a collection of attributes to suit a purpose. These can be dimensions, materials, properties, performance, and so on, which are usually, though not invariably, measurable and expressible in

1

units. The measurements can be absolute, fundamental or fairly straightforward in physical terms, such as those for length, composition, strength, and speed; or require relative frames of reference or arbitrary standards, such as those for colour and noise. Sometimes, the attributes require a subjective norm or non-measurable assessment, as for taste, smell, and, particularly, aesthetic values such as beauty (in the eye of the beholder). — relate to definition of quality

Highest quality. In the context in which the word "quality" usually appears, there is often an understood qualifying adjective as mentioned above and which produces the assumption of excellence of quality. To clarify this before putting it on one side, it can be defined roughly in the following terms: excellence of quality is provided by that collection of attributes which serves the required purpose to the highest degree, and which is independent of the usual restrictions of first cost, shortage of materials, and so on.

Too few things (or services) in the world are readily recognised as the acme of perfection of their kind. Many arrogate to themselves the label "Best in the World," or something similar, but in most cases this label cannot be substantiated and the advertisers rely on the opposite fact, namely that it cannot be disproved. There is something to be said for excellence, ignoring cost; it has great value in terms of morale and even patriotism. There is even a market for it, although this is bound to be limited; let excellence of quality not be dismissed lightly.

Optimum quality. Nevertheless, the great majority of would-be users of products or services are bent on achieving their purposes at the least possible cost. Usually, this also means least possible *first* cost— the "cost of acquisition." Sometimes, however, there is sufficient information available for the user to consider least possible "cost of ownership" during the useful life of the product. This is the total cost including first cost, running cost, cost of maintenance and spares, repairs, as is discussed later (*see page 141*). In either case, optimum quality is, therefore, that collection of attributes which achieves the most "economic" fulfilment of purpose; or which achieves the maximum proportion of the purpose desired for the least expenditure; and can be described as best value for money. It is this quality which should be understood in any general use of the word. With the exception of certain requirements of special or restrictive character, such as may be involved in safety considerations where stipulations for unavoidably

2

high quality or a particular level of quality may be made, the object of the customer for a product or service is to achieve as much as possible for as little as possible cost.

Delivery. Before proceeding further into the subject of quality, a word should be said about delivery. For the overall control can, very roughly, be said to start with good design and end with prompt delivery. (This is an oversimplification to make the point!)

The best product in the world is no use until actually delivered and, therefore, delivery promises must be kept; realistic ones are better than desirable ones. In any case, since the control of quality must be looked upon as a profitable venture, it could not be measured for effectiveness except in relation to ultimate payments by customers. These depend not on quality products, but on *delivered* quality products.

In the author's own experience, there are more customers dissatisfied about delivery than about quality. For while, to the manufacturer, quality is a set of measurable properties as described above, to the customer quality is zero until the product is delivered and put into use. When any proposals for the control of quality are considered by the manufacturer, they must be sufficiently elastic to accommodate all three of the customer's interests: quality, cost, and delivery. No one is going to pay excessively or wait interminably for a specific quality.

Meaning of reliability

"Reliability" is a word whose general implications, like quality, are well known, although perhaps more vaguely, to every user of equipment or services from the simplest to the most complex. It carries implications of trustworthiness, dependability, and availability for use. To the housewife, the reliability of her vacuum cleaner is of the highest importance; its technical degree of efficiency is of little interest. The astonishing thing is that scientists and engineers have always given considerably more attention and comprehensive examination to the latter in all stages of design, development, or testing. The requirements of customers who provide quantitative stipulations very often make great play with the attainment of a specified efficiency, rarely is reliability even mentioned. There is no doubt, however, that had more attention been given in the past to economy than to efficiency, the implications of reliability would have sunk home earlier; for reliability is a powerful factor in economy.

It is a factor in customer satisfaction. The supply of reliable commodities and services is a paying proposition. Those who are involved and concern themselves with the reliability of their company's products are not only helping to improve its current performance and profitability, but also laying the foundations for success in the future. They are taking steps to reduce the costs incurred as a result of unreliability in whatever form. These may be the intrinsic unreliability of the product, in which case costs of replacement or rework, or placation or loss of customer would be involved either at the beginning of the product's life or after an unreasonably short life of satisfactory performance. On the other hand, costs of unreliability could be involved in the activities leading to the product and might be the same as, or include, the costs of non-attainment of quality.

The reduction in these potential losses are only the direct benefits, and they can be measured by fairly straightforward means. Indirectly, and less easily measurable, there are usually benefits which are greater in magnitude. Attention given to reliability sets up a situation and the necessary circumstances in which the satisfied customer will wish to purchase again; this will not only include the same products but also other products of the same background. His satisfaction is an advertisement for the supplier and can often be the cause of gaining new customers. In setting up a policy in relation to reliability activities, the quantitative examinations of the estimated outcome, which are to be used to justify the expenditure, may show direct gains from the various means of reducing unreliability of only a small percentage of the total performance. The indirect gains, such as the possible acquisition of a new order or customer, although less quantifiable, provide an improvement of a higher order of magnitude. These are likely to provide a justification for the policy when there is any doubt in the first case.

Reliability is of especial importance in the case of customers at great distances, and particularly in foreign countries. Here the costs of unreliability, whether they are due to simple quality defects, untimely failure, or reduction in promised performance, are much greater. Placation, rectification, even after-sales service of whatever nature, are always considerably more expensive than corresponding local activities. The nuisance to the customer is also substantially higher. In these cases, therefore, it is doubly necessary to ensure reliability. Indeed, it has sometimes been found, in a situation in which a particular level of costs or degree of unreliability is accepted as tolerable, that sales in a particular area are not worth seeking as being prohibitively expensive to achieve—or perhaps of borderline dubiety. Removal or reduction in costs of unreliability in all forms can be the cause of opening up new markets coming into this category. At the least they will make the supplier more competitive in absolute terms in existing markets.

Limitations of guarantees. Guarantees are usually associated with both quality and reliability. They are intended to mollify the customer in the case of an immediate quality defect by means of repair or replacement. In the case of inadequate performance or life within a stipulated period after purchase, they provide for compensation which varies from replacement downwards, according to the degree of loss (and sometimes sophistication and insistence of the customer). They may be provided automatically by the supplier or required by the terms of contract laid down by the customer, who may also hedge them round with penalty and bonus clauses relating to such features as delivery, quality, reliability, and performance.

Generally, they are an earnest of the manufacturer's confidence in his product and his control of processes. Nevertheless, they are no *substitute* for reliability and must never be considered so by either party. A passenger flying across the Atlantic Ocean would derive neither comfort nor satisfaction from the knowledge that, should an engine of the aircraft fail or drop off, it would be replaced free by the reputable makers.

At a more mundane level, let us suppose a housewife has ordered a suite of lounge furniture from a highly respected store. In due course it is delivered and, perhaps with some difficulty and disturbance, installed in her lounge. To her chagrin, the first time she entertains guests (partly to show it off), a spring, not adequately anchored, pops through the covers and tears someone's dress. Her day is ruined; she telephones the store manager in anger and he is desolate. With the high reputation of his organisation at stake he assures "madame" that the suite will be replaced free and that compensation will be paid in relation to the guest's dress.

A few days later, after waiting in the house for some time, in spite of wishing to go shopping, the van arrives and the procedure of removing the faulty suite—with possible foot marks on the carpet and an occasional bump against the wallpaper—takes place. For some time she is without her suite and then the same procedure takes place with the new or repaired suite. At the end of all this it is true that the

5

customer may have achieved satisfaction, but she has also suffered nuisances and side effects, deprival of use, the ruination of her social event. One could argue that the charge of deprival of use is hardly fair since she had no suite immediately beforehand, but this argument certainly would not hold if the example referred to the installation of, say, production equipment intended to start producing to a plan at a given or specified time.

Thus, although guarantees may be intended to display to the customer the manufacturer's acceptance of responsibility for the quality and reliability of his goods, they are not to be considered as an alternative to the concepts of "right first time," which are the only means of really ensuring satisfaction.

What is provided by reliability. To the ordinary user of equipment, reliability can be defined in the terms of a simple statement of need such as: "it must work as it is supposed to do whenever I require it to do so, for a reasonable length of time." This is a perfectly feasible requirement of reliability and—should it be possible to elaborate it with quantities identifying what is meant by "work as it is supposed to do," enumerating "whenever I require it to do so," and stating what is meant exactly by "a reasonable length of time"—it would become an exact definition of reliability requirement. The user would certainly accept and understand that, in return for the provision of that reliability and possibly to help to maintain it, a counter-requirement of the supplier might be that it was necessary to keep the equipment clean, to lubricate it at stated intervals, and, possibly, to replace certain minor components which wear out at other intervals. On the other hand, of course, the user, while accepting these necessities of maintenance, could not be blamed for seeking the same degree of reliability from competitors' products which, perhaps, require less attention in order to achieve and maintain it.

The article or equipment would be expected to work reasonably well—minor changes in efficiency not being considered important—in the sense of achieving the objectives. If it were a vacuum cleaner, this would mean cleaning the carpets with no undue increase in time spent or effort in doing so. It might be required, say, three times a week on average and, for the expenditure of that amount of money in purchasing it, be expected to "last" or give no trouble for perhaps five years. If only users could be persuaded to make these stipulations, even in the form of crude estimates, the practices required for the achievement of reliability would become more widespread and common-place.

So far, reference has been made to an ordinary user. In the case of the "sophisticated" user—the expression is used in no way derogatory to the first—the definition of reliability would be more substantial. It could be in the form "it must not fall below a certain level of perform-ance over a stipulated time when operated in the conditions indicated." This would be amplified with quantities such that the first requirement was to incur no more than a fixed number of failures per stated period, and adding that no two of these should be more frequent than so many hours apart, nor any occupy a longer time than a given number of minutes in rectification. The second requirement would be to maintain the performance—expressed in object achieved, rate of work or produc-tion, output of energy, or whatever—for a life of so many thousand hours of operation or years of alternately operating and resting. The third requirement would be the necessity for these stipulations to be maintained in a stated atmospheric environment or with particular conditions of supply of power, water, heat, or materials—or with skilled or non-skilled workers; or with no easy access to repair facilities.

Reliability could well be defined in purely economic terms, for it has been stated as a factor in economy. It ought to be perfectly acceptable to consider a statement to the effect that "it must not cost more than a total sum of money over so many years, having regard to all elements of cost including, not only the initial or first cost, but also the costs of transporting, installation, running, maintenance, spares, repairs, labour, and so on." In particular cases, the total costs could also include those attributable to loss of production during breakdown, and even consequential losses. However, great care must be taken in defining these closely and also the conditions in which they can be measured fairly, as well as ensuring that they are reasonable in relation to the contract between consumer and supplier.

In general, therefore, it can be seen that definitions of reliability can, or ought to, be as much requirements of products (and services) as the actual quality attributes, such as dimensions, speed, and strength, that are usually specified. That this has not often been the case, may well be because the physical requirements are or have been more easily quanti-fied. Nevertheless, the prospective user or purchaser has a very wide choice of means of expressing his requirements of reliability, and it can be inferred from the above that attempts to do so cannot but help in creating gradual improvement.

7

Economic rewards of Q and R activities

It is proposed to discuss a series of attitudes and activities of which many can be seen to be plain common sense. More complex techniques which might follow from these are comparatively secondary as far as top management is concerned; in any case they will vary from company to company, and from product to product. The adoption of a Q and R atmosphere throughout an organisation is, however, a universal requirement with benefits which can be seen because the basis of the attitude is the absolute necessity for involvement and quantification—of actually measuring what is going on.

The rewards, or potential rewards, of further involvement will become obvious at first measurement. If they are low, as in a well-run company already practising Q and R—whether described as such or not is immaterial—then the need to invest further money on increasing the rewards may be a dubious advantage. If they are high, it will become as clear as daylight that money judiciously spent on Q and R will be returned many times.

A survey of a large number of firms some five years ago gave the total costs of not having the proper Q and R activities as lying between 12–20 per cent of the turnover—that is, the same order as the total profit. For the Conference of the National Productivity Year in 1963, a sample of some 2000 firms, spread throughout the United Kingdom and consisting of a wide variety of manufacturing interests, was examined for their provisions for the simplest forms of control of quality. The results showed that:

14% had good control.
48% had fair control.
29% had poor control.
9% had bad or no control.

It was deduced from this that about one-third were probably losing money and reputation because of inadequate attention to quality activities; and that only about one-seventh could be said to have sufficiently high standards of practice as not to be able to benefit significantly from further attention to these.

At the same conference, it was estimated that defective manufacture alone was costing British industry some £400 millions a year. To this figure could be added the cost to the customers themselves of having, because of unreliability in one form or other, to provide additional

8

supervision, unnecessary and extra maintenance, or more spares. This was estimated to be a sum not less than twice as large and probably of the order of £1000 millions a year. Thus, it can be seen, even allowing for the crudeness of these figures, that there are opportunities for extremely large rewards. Indeed, it was claimed that the national product could be raised by about 5 per cent and wastage halved with little effort other than attention to the appropriate management attitudes.

In the same year, inspired by interest in the subject of reliability, an investigation was made of the cost of unreliability in the fighting services. It was stated that this amounted to a very large proportion of their total budget. A Royal Air Force report [P C Cleaver, *The Cost of Unreliability to the RAF*, Symposium of the Society of Environmental Engineers, March 1963], indicated that the cost of unreliability was about 40 per cent of the annual air estimates and that increases in reliability of its equipment could easily produce savings in terms of tens of millions of pounds each year.

At a conference ["Reliability": a conference organised by the NCB, Brighton, May 1966] which was a preliminary event to the Quality and Reliability Year beginning in October, a speaker for the Fleet Air Arm [Commander J A Breedon, RN, *The Cost of Unreliability*], whose unreliability problems were not dissimilar to those of the NCB, stated that maintenance cost the FAA £50 millions a year of which unreliability cost some £15 millions a year. To achieve a 95 per cent chance of successfully completing a single sortie mission on the existing reliability figures demanded the dispatch of two aircraft.

For the NCB itself, at the same conference, it was shown that sample analyses of measurements made during machine utilisation studies, indicated that an increase in availability of 10 per cent, or some 15–20 minutes every shift, would improve the Board's finances by £5–6 millions a year. The author's own personal experience of the effects of the application of controls described earlier, concerns the development of fire-resistant conveyor belting for the NCB. At the beginning of the project in 1955–6 the total installation of conveyor belting in service was 26 million feet; this rose to 29 million feet in 1958–9 and then fell slowly to about 25 million feet in 1964–5. In this period the effect of the application of Q and R principles was an improvement in quality, measured as life in service, from an overall average value of just over two years to over three and a half years, a 75 per cent increase. This resulted in savings of the order of £10 millions a year in that one

9

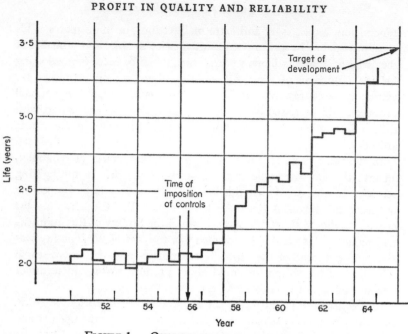

FIGURE 1   QUALITY IMPROVEMENT IN ACTION

An example of the improvement in quality of fire-resistant
conveyor belting in the National Coal Board. The application
of Q and R principles from 1956 led to a steady increase of life
in service and the saving of millions of pounds.

commodity. Figure 1 shows the increase in life over the period described.

It could be argued, as indeed it was at the NCB Conference, that
economies to the user might be to the supplier's disadvantage. After
listening to a catalogue of the savings to be expected from the supply
of better equipment, one impatient manufacturer asked directly: "What's
in it for me if I supply such good equipment that you buy less or at
lower frequency?" The answers to this difficult question are, however,
easily available and can be supported by evidence from organisations
whose success is a result of the adoption of Q and R activities. They
include the following:

1   The supply of reliable equipment retains existing customers
     and gains new ones.
2   Turnover is not as important as profit.
3   The introduction of activities which lead to greater reliability
     results in greater productivity.

10

4   Customers can be persuaded to pay more for *demonstrably* better equipment.

5   In cases where purchasing is on some basis other than first cost —for example, by paying for life—the benefits are to both parties.

6   Prestige and reputation are enhanced.

The above examples of potential and actual rewards indicate the scope of Q and R activities when applied by the right attitude in management. Procedures intended to improve profitability are automatically more efficacious when based on an organisation in which losses due to lack of quality or to unreliability have first been minimised.

The future in industry. In industry generally, rapid moves are being made to increase the degree of automation or mechanisation (in the broadest terms). Machines, equipment, and systems are becoming more complex and expensive. They are being used more intensively (because of their costs) and the costs of a breakdown or failure for whatever reason are becoming higher. Expensive equipment standing idle for any length of time is a serious problem, which can be solved by instituting requirements for higher reliability and greater effectiveness in new generations of equipment. Longer and more continuous operation will be dependent on greater availability to operate. Unless reliability is increased, the first results of attempts at more intensive use will be more breakdowns and the necessity for more maintenance, repairs, and spares.

At the same time, the reduction in manpower measured in terms of specific production criteria will mean fewer men available for such activities as correction, putting things right, and trouble shooting. The greater the reliability, the less the demand for these. This will also bring additional rewards in that the less the necessity for being in contact with equipment, the fewer the number of accidents or the greater the overall safety.

The rewards of Q and R activities will be seen when, as a matter of routine practice, the costs of not having those appropriate to any organisation, will be in constant measurement and never accepted subjectively as unpleasant facts of life. Management will then have taken the first giant step to increasing the effectiveness, productivity, and profitability of their organisations—and thence of the whole country.

11

Two

Basic Requirements of a
Q and R Policy

Management has to be inspired to the acceptance of Q and R procedures as profitable and not "gimmicky" activities—to the examination of the potentialities of these in relation to the balance sheet. The term "quality control" is too often bandied about with techniques which savour vaguely of pure inspection and which are clouded with the corresponding jargon such as "scatter," "mean square," and "sampling." Some firms are complacent in having an inspector or an inspection department and assuming that this alone is quality control. Recognising the need to explain the wider requirements, experts in this field have decided to differentiate by the use of new terms such as "total quality control." These, in the author's opinion, defeat the object by appearing to confirm that, while quality control by itself is a specific technique, there are fringe or ancilliary activities not related to, but having an effect on, quality control. This is why it is preferable to talk about "the control of quality" and it is to be assumed that any reference elsewhere to quality control is in the context of control of quality and not of a specific technique, unless this is obviously intended.

It is important to put down the sequence of activities in an organisation which have an effect on quality and which, therefore, have to be examined in any considerations for the overall control of quality. These were briefly discussed at the National Conference of the British Quality and Reliability Year which took place at Blackpool in November 1966 [*Profiting by Quality and Reliability*, Report of National Conference 1966 with forty-one case studies, NCQR, London EC4]. The author, who acted as rapporteur for manufacture, took fifteen case studies in industries varying from aircraft to clothing and examined the practices necessary. There emerged the following generalisations which seemed to summarise the requirements for the control of quality.

Ascertaining requirements of customer or user

How many manufacturers or suppliers stop to think deeply about this "market orientation" which is another way of saying the same thing? If the customer has a want or a need to be satisfied, he must be sold what he actually wants, not what the supplier *thinks* he wants, and not that which is near enough to what he wants—all, of course, at a satisfactory price. Many companies overlook this elementary fact and make products or provide services, on the assumption that later, when a customer selects one of these, then that is indeed what he wants. It may be near enough, or it may "do," or it may be comparable with a competitor's offering; but it is rare to find suppliers taking the trouble to investigate the real and exact needs.

Sometimes a customer who is not able to stipulate accurately what he wants or who has not given much thought to his requirements, can merely produce or refer to a competitor's product, asking for a similar one to be made. If questioned, he will usually admit, however, that he wants it cheaper or better in some way—for why else would he come?

So it is necessary to draw out a potential customer to explain his full need, in the context of value for money, even when this is based on an existing product. Does it require greater strength or higher speed— or increased wearing properties? No one-sided assumptions should be made. He should be warned against "frills"—that is, unnecessary elaborations which usually increase cost to no useful effect—and thus help to make, say, the designer's task easier. Careful approaches in this manner ultimately permit the manufacturer to perform "value engineering," or design as a result of a study of what it is wanted to achieve, no more, no less.

Some customers fall into special categories. These are usually the larger ones—for example, the nationalised industries and the so-called "sophisticated" industries such as those involved in the manufacture of aircraft. In these cases, it is not so much a case of drawing out information from the customer, as the reverse. He is usually equipped with adequate facilities to make the most comprehensive stipulations to his supplier. These may include requirements of safety or performance imposed on the customer by another body or by the law. Situations of this kind are relatively easy to handle by the setting-up of correct supplier/user relationships to determine the detailed needs.

The practice of making market surveys to assess existing or future requirements can be extremely useful not only in determining sales policies, but also in the more fundamental needs of groups of potential customers in terms of design detail. Even in this case, however, a check-back with individuals is necessary from time to time, in the recognition that organised measures taken to ensure the entire satisfaction of the customer are of basic economic significance.

Embodiment of requirements in design

When there is a clear understanding of the requirements, it may still be necessary to consider the possibilities of fulfilling them. Sometimes a manufacturer can make important suggestions about methods of manufacture, availability, and nature of materials, factors affecting cost and delivery. Perhaps all the requirements cannot be achieved except at great cost; a minor modification could have a disproportionately large effect on the price. As a result, it may finally be necessary to compromise and accept a variation of the requirements. This must be mutually agreed and recorded before taking steps to produce a design.

The design is the proposal for the embodiment in a "thing" of the ultimately agreed requirements. Sometimes it is desirable for the supplier and user to see a prototype of what was hitherto vaguely described; and sometimes the original requirements were expressed only in terms of the purpose to be achieved, without stipulating the means of achievement—the "hardware." The design procedure may be relatively simple, as in the event that an existing or standard product can be used or modified; on the other hand, it may involve a completely new departure.

The requirements have to be met by the "thing," so it is necessary to perform those tests or go through those procedures which will demonstrate this fact and ensure that they are indeed met. More often than not, adjustments are needed to produce the achievement and these processes, repeated as necessary, should all be considered as part of the design stage. It is important, in some instances, for the customer to involve or interest himself in the prototype and its testing until he is satisfied that his original needs, or the mutually agreed modified stipulations, have been achieved (or indeed that they cannot be, economically, or otherwise).

Specifying

Having arrived at a design which, by means of a prototype and testing, has been shown to be suitable or acceptable, this must be "fixed" by specification. Accuracy and unambiguity are very important here, as are the necessities for including not only characteristics but also the requirements and criteria for the testing and the performance desired to achieve the purpose. Unfortunately, the great majority of existing specifications are merely concerned with calling for particulars and not means. There is sometimes a confusion between the words standard and specification. Asking for a specification may result in the production of a drawing or formula showing simply the primary requirements of dimensions or qualities and, sometimes, materials. For the specification to play its absolutely basic role in the whole chain of procedures which add up to the control of quality, it must be constructed with great care. (*See Chapter 5.*)

Proving the specification

It is one thing for a person to write a specification and another for someone else to make, to that specification, a prototype embodying the original intentions. It is still another, however, to guarantee that, from the specification, the manufacture of more than one article or the repetition of a stipulated service, will always fulfil the requirements. The first person may have made assumptions or have had an understanding which appears to him to be implicit in his statement. This may be read by someone else with a different interpretation. In the case of more than one article, and especially where components of an assembly may be involved, special precautions are necessary. Each unit of one particular component must be capable of assembly with each unit of every other component involved. In other words, if a machine is made up of parts A and B, all As must be capable of fitting with all Bs.

If, because of inherent variations in materials, or dimensions, A may lie in the range $A \pm a$ and, similarly, B in the range $B+b$, it has to be checked that the worst possible extremes can still produce the desired objectives. These may be constructions of $A+a$ fitted to $B-b$, or $A-a$ to $B+b$. It is a useful exercise, especially in mass production, to select all worst possible cases of matching or mating—the smallest peg in the largest hole, and the largest peg in the smallest hole—and in this way to construct the possible extremes of quality. Some manufacturers insist on this procedure before embarking on an expensive production programme, and there have been cases in which it has been found that the extreme cases cannot even be *assembled* let alone achieve a desired performance or effect. Obviously the specification has then to be re-examined in relation to such features as tolerances on both dimensions and also performance.

On the other hand, if it is too expensive to make all extremes fit, the manufacturer may be prepared to take a small risk of replacement as a more economic procedure.

The same arguments hold when the process equipment involved in the production, through wear and tear or for any other reason, changes in its capability to produce to the requirements. Since this is normally a slow and continuous effect, periodical checks are necessary. These can be the examination of the extremes of production as above, or by direct measurements of the equipment.

Manufacturer's acceptance of responsibility for compliance with requirements

At the outset of any negotiations, the responsibilities for the various activities should be clearly placed. The responsibility for quality is a particular case, but this requires an examination of two aspects of what is usually covered by the one word, quality. The supplier is always responsible for the "quality of conformance," that is ensuring that what he produces is consistently compliant in full with the agreed stipulations in whatever form and by whomever made. These could include specifications or Approved features. (*See Chapter 9.*) On the other hand, the "quality of the design" may or may not be the supplier's responsibility. If the customer made comprehensive stipulations or provided a full specification, then clearly he is responsible for the suitability for purpose, on the understanding that the manufacturer conforms. This is often the case with big user organisations which, for their own purposes, prefer to control the design aspect of quality.

Where the supplier has produced the design for a purpose that the customer may or may not have indicated, he is responsible for both the quality of design or performance and also the compliance with the characteristics of the embodiment. A customer's interests are best served, therefore, by ensuring that the supplier he chooses is one who fully understands his responsibilities in the above contexts. The supplier cannot throw off his responsibilities because the customer had indicated that he was satisfied with the arrangements for the control of quality, or because the customer or his representative (inspector) pays visits to ensure that all is well. In particular, he cannot lean on the fact that he has been approved as a supplier by some external body.

Most companies would, of course, robustly deny any failure to accept responsibility (indeed balance sheet results may well depend on this), but it would appear from investigations that the acceptance is more often implicit than clearly defined or formalised. On the other hand, there are honourable exceptions where the acceptance of responsibility goes as far as the performing of audits of the degree of success achieved in satisfying customers, in protecting their interests, and, at the same time, in enhancing the company's prestige. Other exceptions are in those industries which have statutory and other high responsibilities for safety, and so on, thrust upon them.

The responsibility cannot be thrown off by the type of guarantee which, in effect, limits the customer's rights. All that the customer should require for his protection is a dated receipt or similar record of the purchase. The purchase price itself should not be of undue significance unless it has been reduced particularly for an acceptable (by the customer) reduction in quality, or a defect tolerable (by the customer).

It is useful for the customer to require the assurance of acceptance of responsibility for quality (quality assurance) in documentary form, but it is rather a waste of time and paper if this merely repeats to the customer what, after all, has been undertaken in the particular order or contract. (Without order or contract, however, a statement of quality can go some way to provide the information required when there is no specification involved.) In the case of a specification being part of the contractual arrangements between supplier and customer, a document that states that the goods or supplies comply is not enough. It is suggested, therefore, that suppliers should volunteer, and customers should seek, further information in such a document. This could be a reference to testing being continually performed, with test records and values being available to the customer for perusal and check if required.

Finally, however, it must be stated that when it is clear that what is being supplied is in fact of the correct quality and consistency and completely satisfactory, it is obvious that the supplier has accepted his responsibility in a proper manner. It may then be pointless, and sometimes a nuisance and an unnecessary expense, to seek formal assurances of responsibility.

Inspection

The level of quality having been determined by the sum of the attributes stipulated or specified, the consistency or uniformity of quality has to be maintained by formal processes and techniques. The results of these largely, though not entirely, come under the responsibility of inspection that is dealt with at some length later, since it is one of the most important features in the control of quality.

The customer should not, however, confuse inspection with the control of quality of which the former is one part and which we are now discussing in its various steps. Some companies label inspection as "quality control" and the inspection department as the "quality control department." Besides being wrong, for inspection is a part of control of quality, attempts to make quality everybody's business (managing director to floor sweeper) can be defeated if there is a specific department labelled "quality" to which the buck can be passed.

A "one hundred per cent inspection" may well ensure that the customer never receives a defective product, but it may be equivalent to a process of separating good from bad at the end of a production line. This causes the customer to pay a price which includes the cost of the production of the defectives he *doesn't* receive. Inspection and allied quality control techniques should aim at increasing the proportion of good things, and at becoming a checking not a separating process. The result of good inspection is higher productivity in terms of lower prices per unit and more good units produced in the same time. Since it is allied to productivity in this way, inspection has to pay for itself and, before introducing a single inspector into a system, it would be highly negligent if the one responsible could not justify this move by indicating a probable saving by so doing.

Advice to customer

Obviously for the customer to achieve full satisfaction, it is necessary in some instances to advise him on the optimum use and possible limitations of the product; to instruct him on lubrication, maintenance, overhaul, or on mundane matters such as cleanliness. Where a value of reliability features formally in the negotiations, it is of particular importance to describe the exact assumptions, conditions of use, environment, and so on, leading the designer to the value claimed. The customer might then be able to improve on that set of conditions and achieve higher reliability, or at least understand the reasons for not attaining the value stated.

Large customers rely substantially on advice from suppliers in the form of, or to be incorporated in, information bulletins, handbooks, codes of practice, or specifications, which can be circulated to all concerned. In these cases, there is usually a special relationship between customer and supplier. On the other hand, in the case of the supply of, say, a domestic appliance, instructions have to be carefully designed in the form of a compromise between the too technical and the completely non-technical. The former may confuse a customer and the latter not satisfy him. Advice to customers, therefore, must be carefully drawn up with the customer in view and possibly tailored to suit different markets.

Feed of information from operations to manufacturer

Every company has, at one time or other, to deal with complaints, provided the customer takes the trouble to complain rather than secretly nurse a grievance and purchase elsewhere in future. Those organisations which provide a follow-up service or with associated servicing arrangements, can accumulate operational experience. A representative of the civil aircraft industry recently wrote: "The customer has bought the aircraft to operate as a commercial proposition and any failure . . . to meet its specified performance will affect his margin of profit. He will not keep this information to himself." Records are kept and added to reports of deficiencies in production, usually available through testing or inspection.

Code of complaints. Apart from these, however, not enough companies take active steps to obtain customer experience, which can be done by means of any sales organisation, internal and external, and directly from the customer. Throughout an organisation a very simple code of complaints can be known and used by all those in a position to add information. In the first instance, this need only point to the general nature of a complaint, be it delivery, quality, or whatever. At frequent intervals the summary should be circulated to those responsible for the necessary corrective activities, and copied to high authority as a means of communicating the current state of affairs.

A typical arrangement might be as shown in Appendix 1 in which four main headings, Delivery, Quality, Customer Orientation, and

Miscellaneous, have been used. These have been broadly split up into sub-headings and finally into details. Each part of the organisation that is concerned with complaints—that is nearly everybody—must make themselves familiar with at least the main headings and sub-heading codes. Suitable printed forms with boxes for the sub-headings D1, D2, Q1, and so on, can be issued to those accumulating evidence. The forms should indicate the period concerned and the part of the organisation involved (Sales Region, Internal Sales Office, or Production Department) and must be collected and summarised in simple form in similar boxes for the quick digestion of top management who can see at a glance to what field of activity to direct their attention. In many cases, this sort of control can be used not only to isolate those who are not doing their jobs properly, but, in particular, to provide information as to the adequacy of the staff organisation, where there is superfluity, and where insufficient strength.

Checklist of steps. To sum up, therefore, these are the fundamental steps or sequences on which the successful control of quality can be based:

1 Consultation with the customer as to his exact requirements.
2 Design and development.
3 The writing of specifications to include the means of ensuring performance, quality, and reliability.
4 Examination of the processes for capability to produce to requirements (specification).
5 Formal procedure of acceptance by the manufacturer of responsibility for quality.
6 Inspection as an important part of the control of quality.
7 Advice and instruction to the customer.
8 Taking positive steps to acquire the valuable experience of the user.

When organisational moves have been implemented in these different activities and when the appropriate responsibilities have been placed for them, it can then be said that there is overall control of quality.

Organisation for overall control of quality

The establishment of proper controls for quality and the measurement of what is going on (and why) also provide the true basis for general development where this is required. When information is collected and carefully utilised to increase the proportion of good products, this is itself an increase in productivity. It also provides data pointing to areas where modifications may be necessary, or will bring an improvement in the product. Any organisation that is set up to collect this information in a factual and rationalised manner, and to communicate it to those concerned with the relevant activities, is a control organisation.

Linkage with the customer. The most important feature of such an organisation apart from the intrinsic requirements of speed and efficiency in collecting and operating on the proper information, is its linkage with other organisations concerned with the same product. Thus, in the case of the manufacturer, his internal organisation must link up at various points with his customer or *his* organisation, so that usage data is put into circuit. In the case of a user, the linkage must be with the manufacturer(s) so that design, development, and control information can be fed into optimum usage. Broadly speaking, therefore, internal organisations ought to be parts of a larger one concerned not merely with either manufacture or use, but with both. This can only be achieved if, in the first instance, the prime considerations are the purpose to be fulfilled and the product itself, not the people concerned. It is what happens to the product, from the ideas or conception stage to the end of its life in use, which determines development and enables control at the appropriate phases in its history. Such a history is shown in Figure 2 in which one half of the cycle depicts the above stages from idea to use, and the other extracts the data in order to make adjustments, or to develop. As will be seen, it is possible for the customer or user to take part in all the stages other than manufacture. Similarly, the manufacturer can involve himself in all but actual usage. In some cases the customer provides the specification and the design, and also has a checking procedure. In others, the manufacturer may have to advise the customer as to what he wants in regard to his purpose, and then prepare specification, and so on. The feed of information takes place from usage to the source of knowledge, customer or manufacturer (preferably both), and this is used for development, causing activity through the specification, design, and such stages, which result in improved operational parameters. (Using the language of cybernetics, the "feed-back" is actually the flow of accumulated experience into the product for its improvement, but common usage refers to it as the accumulation from operations to source. The choice is not very material

21

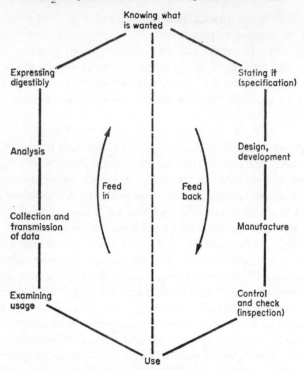

Knowing what
is wanted

Expressing
digestibly

Stating it
(specification)

Analysis

Design,
development

Feed
in

Feed
back

Collection and
transmission
of data

Manufacture

Examining
usage

Control
and check
(inspection)

Use

FIGURE 2   ORGANISATION FOR CONTROL OF
QUALITY: PRODUCT BASED

A suggested arrangement of the processes through which a
product passes. Both manufacturer and user have an equal
interest in many of these.

provided that the meaning is clear.) The constant accumulation of data
in this way serves many purposes, but the two most important ones
are:

1   To assist in the prediction of the behaviour of the product or
       system.
2   Gradually to establish an increasing standard of behaviour.

It is true without exception that setting up an interlinked organisation
of this nature with the object of quantifying behaviour, measuring what
is happening, assessing costs, and making all this information available
whenever required, leads to general improvement. Referring back to

22

the general steps required for the control of quality, it will also be seen that such an organisation makes possible all these steps in a natural and sequential manner.

Internal organisation. The internal organisations of either (large) user or manufacturer are less easy to describe in general terms, for they can vary according to product, size of company, and so on, and can be simple to the point of non-existence in a very small company, or complex in a widespread group. The basis of an organisation for the control of quality is its effect on economy. Pressures from a large customer to set up a system for the control of quality, appoint a quality manager, chief inspector, and so on, must be considered mutually in the light of the present state of quality of the product. If by setting up or increasing the size of a system there will be gains as a result, then it is obvious that such a system is an advantage. (In making estimates, the possible gain of new custom has to be considered.) If, however, the quality and consistency of the product is already satisfactory, as for example in the case of a one-man (craftsman) company, it would merely be an additional unjustified cost to take further special steps.

[There is a salutory story of a large organisation which decided that the setting up of a special quality organisation was a necessary move in view of the less-than-best quality level and inconsistency prevailing. In due course, a separate new building, with "Quality Control Department" over the door, was put up and staffed with a handful of graduates and technicians. This was about a quarter of a mile away from the main factory.

The quality control soon got under way, with more intercommunication between the special staff (*vide* Parkinson's Law) than with the works. However, the quality and consistency of the product hardly improved.

One day a visiting foreign plenipotentiary and important potential customer was shown over the works and spent some time in this department. He was so impressed with the *steps* taken in the control of quality that large orders were forthcoming! (There is a moral here.) The law of diminishing returns holds here as elsewhere.]

Thus, the first consideration, of interest to both user and manufacturer, is whether the introduction of a control system, or the modification of an existing one would improve the economy. This might be achieved either by a lower price for existing quality—where improvement in control gave increased productivity—or the same (or a higher) price for still higher quality. Purchasers, in particular, must be made aware that higher quality, requiring greater control, might involve higher first costs. Systems, plus accompanying activity, documentation, and so on, are costly, must be justified and have to be paid for.

Having made out a case which justifies the setting up or enlargement of a system, however, there are certain generalised principles which are appropriate to all systems in internal organisations, big and small. These are:

1 To ensure that quality and simple output are not in conflict, as would be the case if both were the executive responsibility of one man. (*See "Inspection," pages 82–3*).

2 Not to confine overall quality responsibilities to the quality system, but to make everyone aware of his part in the process.

3 To provide rapid communication between all interested parties and linkage with the customer (or manufacturer) by means of appropriate staff—technical personnel talking to technical personnel, and so on.

4 To note that the control of consistency of quality can only be done at the point of production, not from a distance.

5 While inspection may be all that is necessary, to note that it is only part of the control of quality, which usually requires complementary measures elsewhere.

6 To associate the whole system with an audit—for example, by cost and works accountancy—to monitor its effectiveness in economic terms.

As an example of a useful type of system in a large organisation, one could have a quality manager at the same level as departmental managers to whom he would be a consultant in regard to quality activities in departments. While they would be responsible to a production executive, he would report to, say, a senior technical executive, and also have ultimate access, in the event of conflict, to the top—that is, to the managing director. Quality personnel, as such, working in departments would have technical responsibilities under the quality manager, but administrative responsibilities to the departmental manager.

The chief inspector would report to the quality manager; or if they were one and the same, however titled, to the senior technical executive. Where it is considered advisable to have specific quality responsi-

bility at high level—for example, by the presence of a quality director—
the right communication with technical personnel must be established
so that there need be no clash between the particular controls of quality
and routine technical servicing of departments.

The above suggestions, while applying only to large organisations in
which the economic benefit has been demonstrated, can be boiled down
to very simple terms in a smaller one, provided that the generalised
principles enumerated above obtain.

Three

Human Contribution to Quality

Successful day-to-day operation of an organisation in stable production requires a flow of relevant information. When it includes any necessary warning signals to permit corrective action if the otherwise routine situation moves into jeopardy, it becomes control of quality and the techniques are the same, whether it is so named or not. The policy which created this stable operation is well tried and its results predictable.

Company objectives and the background to Q and R activities

The best organisations have, in addition, a dynamic sense of purpose and are always in a state of flux, the throes of development. This generates new products or new methods. In these cases the operations represent the implementation of a policy, not so well tried because of being in a regime of change. It is an even greater necessity here to set up similar controls which now provide:

1   An assurance of quality consistency and warning signals for corrective action where necessary—as before.
2   The information which enables the review of the degree of success of the policy by comparing measured results with objectives.
3   The facilities for gear-changing—that is, adjustment of policy parameters (time and speed).

Control information which only relates to output, has been recognised as merely a first approximation to productivity measurement, which

26

requires a closer criterion—output of good. Thus, the question "how are we doing?" can only be answered by measurement of degree of "how-ness," in fact, quality. The essence of all quality and reliability procedures is this quantification of level and proportion of good. So it can be seen that *basic* Q and R activities, the proper conditions for development, and optimum production procedures are really one and the same thing.

It will be found, on delving deeper into the subject, that all activities coming into the broad sphere of Q and R are those of management for profit. Conversely, moves to optimise profit automatically lead to a policy which, at foundation, is essentially Q and R.

Top management requires to know (up to date and accurately) two things:

1   What is actually going on.
2   What customers think about it.

The first is the measurement of productivity (good output) and profitability. It also includes the information needed to improve these. The second involves Q and R aspects more fully, in that it is necessary to take positive steps to measure the degree of customer satisfaction. The quality is a function of the fitness for his purpose, the reliability is the trustworthiness in continuing to fulfil that purpose. Both sets of information are the responsibility of middle management who take all possible actions to acquire them in rational form. They know that they are sources not only of Q and R data as such, but also of the most valuable kind of development information. It is in this way that areas of improvement in productivity or in customer satisfaction are revealed and the bases for objectives isolated. For these reasons, the success of top management depends on:

1   Establishing the correct policy.
2   Causing it to be implemented by staff fully qualified and trained to understand the significance of the policy.
3   Agreement as to the part each one plays in aiming for main objectives of the policy.

These are, in fact, the ways of optimising the work of chief executives, who can construct for themselves a checklist which covers all these points. This would vary from one organisation to another but would include the following points.

Checklist for good organisation.

1   Each position is filled by the best possible man who is the most qualified in all respects.
2   His duties and responsibilities are described accurately and unambiguously, and recorded.
3   He is given full authority corresponding to those responsibilities.
4   He is given all necessary facilities and training.
5   Work and activities within his responsibilities are delegated to him.
6   He is helped by decisive action, taken speedily, by his senior.
7   Decisions, aimed to give best outcome, must be based on all available information.
8   Errors are never perpetuated.
9   "Sacred cows" are kept in periodical review.
10   Absence, for any reason, causes minimum disturbance.
11   The outcome of decisions is prejudged and prerecorded.
12   Communication, paper work, and so on, are simplified to the absolute necessary minimum.
13   Time saving is usually more profitable than money saving.
14   All activities are examined as to effect on balance sheet.

Operating in a background constructed on this sort of basis is good organisation and the proper setting for Q and R activities.

Middle management responsibility

As far as middle management responsibility for quality and reliability is concerned, some aspects do not appear to be directly relevant. Nevertheless, any Q and R techniques leading to increase of profit, or such benefits, can only operate successfully in the right organisation and with proper communications all down the management chain. Those procedures which appear to be routine have to be treated by an active, not a passive attitude. Efficient top management cannot operate or rely on *assumptions* that middle management are actually performing their proper activities. This leads to similar assumptions all down the line: departmental managers assuming that foremen are exactly performing all the necessary duties; and foremen that operators are also doing so. Adequate communications must be set up to ensure that the knowledge of what is actually going on is immediately available, and that each level of activity is monitoring its own performance wherever possible.

Refined techniques in the overall concepts of control (including methods of inspection and statistical quality control) will be found to follow automatically as natural consequentials of wanting to know what is going on. It is not necessary for top management to concern itself with these means, only the ends. It is worse than useless to attempt to introduce techniques until an appropriate set of positive conditions and attitudes such as those above, exist. Indeed such attempts have been known to cause confusion and achieve the opposite result to that intended.

Teamwork. With these matters in mind, it is important for top management to make clear to staff their key responsibilities in relation to where the organisation is going and their own personal roles in the whole movement. In particular, the significance of Q and R activities has to be carefully explained in terms of satisfaction of customers, the gain of new customers, the economy of production and increased competitiveness, the reduction in waste and wasteful activities, and, not least, the increase in profit from which all would benefit.

The necessity for teamwork must be emphasised at the same time as it is ensured that middle management are made aware of general lines of thought and policy, and of their duty to keep themselves informed. The organisation must be such, or must be made such, as to ensure close and facile communication.

Because teamwork is involved it may also be necessary to think in terms of the "league" in which the company is operating—that is, the particular industry. The spirit must be such as to constantly strive for the "championship," to acquire a good name, prestige, and success. Competitions of one form or another should be introduced both internally and externally. These can be based on the personal performances of individuals, or waste reduction between departments, or even efforts to obtain an external award. Recognition of individual, department, or firm, by means of badges, shields, certificates, or flags, should not be despised. For success undoubtedly breeds success through pride in being a member of a successful organisation. Even when certain desirable activities are not possible immediately, or are difficult to achieve, it is important that all efforts must, at least, be in the right direction and each step taken a positive move, however small, towards the known objectives.

Shop floor management

For a Q and R policy to be successful, the responsibilities of a departmental or shop floor manager have to be very clearly defined. They include everything that goes on in his department and are, therefore, only limited by the IN-door and the OUT-door. They do not end merely when a product has been completed, although it is still in the department. The fact that it is finished and ready for going out is not enough. Since his performance cannot be gauged until he has completely discharged his responsibilities, it is his duty to ensure that the product is removed expeditiously as a quality (that is, saleable) unit. Wrong quality will bring it back, or require replacement; all reducing his performance. The fact that the customer's exact requirements have been met, must therefore be checked before release.

Should a final inspection take place other than in that department then, in respect of the particular product, it should be assumed to be a part of the department. Performance can then be based on the position after inspection, but the proper measures taken for the control of quality in production should have made final inspection a mere formality, a check.

A departmental manager's responsibilities are to:

1   Plan.
2   Organise.
3   Co-ordinate.
4   Motivate.
5   Control.

Each step is only successful to the extent of the success of the previous ones. His tools include three Ms.

1   Men.
2   Machines.
3   Materials.

Men. The responsibilities here are to make men act right, do things the proper way. They should have been trained to as high a degree as possible; this is usually considerably higher than first assumed. Then they must be supervised. Supervision requires that the manager, or anyone to whom he may have temporarily delegated the responsibility, acts as a policeman. His physical presence tends to keep all activities within the prescribed requirements and precludes unnecessary activities or time wasting.

This element of personal presence is very important. Some time ago, in an effort to increase the efficiency of fuel utilisation, a large number of coalfired boilers were to be examined for overall efficiency. The figures available from engineers' logs showed that there was room for much improvement and it was proposed to witness a sample number of boiler operations in order to arrive at recommendations. Although this merely involved the presence of an observer who took no part whatever in the proceedings, it was found that the thermal efficiencies of all the observed boilers immediately increased by up to 10 per cent for no apparent reason. The presence of a "policeman" had had the effect of tightening up all operations: furnace doors were not left open, grates were cleaned, gauges were examined, etc. This is the effect of the physical presence of authority.

There have to be times when a manager cannot be present in his department, even though these should be reduced to a minimum. On those occasions, it is his duty to take whatever steps are necessary to ensure proper supervision and control of activities in his absence. These include the obvious ones of full instructions to foremen, and the less obvious ones of similar full instructions to whomever may be in charge of, say, an alternative shift. Any critical information or significant features to be watched must, of course, be accentuated; all measures put into force which will prevent quality failure. There should be no opportunity for one shift to blame another.

Men have to be used in the most efficient and economic manner so that the minimum manpower is needed for any particular operation. A manager must not maintain a labour force greater than necessary to produce at the greatest economy. This is fundamental but an over-simplification. There are many aspects to this consideration which must be carefully examined. First, he must know that the effectiveness of a man is not a constant factor. During initial training he is not only earning little or nothing for his company, but is costing them a considerable amount in providing the facilities. In his career with the firm, he represents an investment unless he has acquired his skill beforehand. Figure 3 shows a hypothetical case of his productive capacity. At first he is a burden costing £OA a week. At the end of a period of training he moves (sometimes gradually) into a job requiring a degree of skill and earns £OB a week for the firm. After a further period, he is deemed to be capable of doing a slightly more important job of effectiveness OC, etc. Sometimes he may be taken off production and trained further, OD for a still higher job, at OE or later OF. A departmental manager must

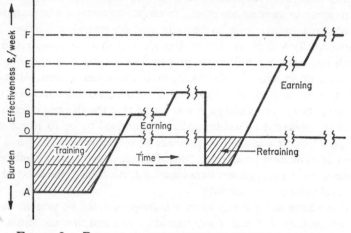

FIGURE 3   RETURN ON INVESTMENT IN OPERATOR TRAINING
A diagrammatic view of the value of an operator at different
periods of time.

make these rationalisations, if necessary in this form, to judge the man's effect on his department's performance.

Having provided training and having instructed in proper activities, the manager also has to make allowances and provisions for absence for any reason, and for possible drift of labour in and out of the industry (loss of investment). When machines are out of action, he may not wish to dismiss trained personnel; while new equipment is being installed it may be necessary to retain operators (usually providing other duties). With the prospect of increased orders, it may be decided to add another shift or, conversely, with a reduction in orders it has to be considered whether this is of such a temporary nature as to justify the retention of men. Thus, management plans for the efficient use of men must be carefully laid down and the assumptions on which these are based, made part of the overall objectives of the company. They must key into the plans of the sales personnel, who must relate orders to efficient production levels, and of the buyers responsible for raw materials supplies. The intermediate departments on whom final operations depend—the engineering or maintenance departments responsible for the installation, upkeep, or repair of production plant —have all to operate in accord.

The most efficient use of men is probably that in which the numbers can be kept stable over long periods, and it pays handsomely to take carefully thought-out measures to achieve this rather than to be constantly having to vary the manpower in relation to a fluctuating programme. It goes without saying that humanitarian and social reasons point to the former.

Effectiveness of the individual can be optimised when he is able to monitor his own performance. Unfortunately, the great majority of workers are totally unaware of the degree to which they are achieving success, what proportion of good or bad work they are producing. Often the results of their work are not established until the end of the production processes or in the final inspection procedure—by which time, much waste of money has been involved.

Management must therefore consider the ways in which operators can be made aware of what is required of their work, and thus introduce control of quality. This can be done by providing guides, patterns, or gauges for the work. Simple pictures, actual examples of diagrams clearly differentiating between what is good and what is bad, what is acceptable and what is not, are extremely powerful tools. That part of a specification relevant to their work can also be prominently displayed for guidance. The relation of their jobs to subsequent processes or to parallel ones in an assembly, also by visual aids or samples, is very important, arousing and maintaining interest, and providing a competitive atmosphere.

This latter is best achieved, however, by the aggregation of records of performance in a department and by displaying these prominently in easily digestible form (such as by pictures or histograms) which, wherever possible, should include targets for achievement and a view of recent history so as to indicate the trend. A "museum" of actual examples of good and bad work is always a considerable benefit.

Machines. Unlike men, machines are normally designed for constant and specific purposes at a uniform rate of effectiveness. They have to be operated, nevertheless, in a sensible manner with some "feel" for the overall capabilities. The designer has built into the machine the required level of performance and reliability based on his own initial design assumptions as to the particular conditions of operation. If these vary in any way, it is not unreasonable to expect the performance and reliability to change. So it is a manager's duty to get to know the optimum operating conditions for his machines. These include the engineering requirements of load and speed; the environmental requirements, atmospheric and otherwise; the avoidance of dust and dirt; the servicing requirements in terms of lubrication or similar routine attention and their frequencies; and the maintenance, overhaul, and spares requirements for longest beneficial life. In addition, he must acquire knowledge of the relation of the machine to the operator for best work and least fatigue. Where some factors are not easily controlled, for example the atmospheric conditions, it is necessary to learn about the possible effect on performance of variations such as ambient temperature and humidity. These should be discussed with the supplier to ensure that the position is fully understood by each side. Then the operators must be instructed in all those aspects which may be of concern to them in getting the best out of the machines.

Information as to reliability and the continuing capability of uniform performance of a machine, is rarely available from a supplier. Nevertheless, it must be sought and, where possible, included in the conditions of sale and purchase; preference given to those suppliers who can provide information in some form or other. In return, arrangements should be made to gather experience about useful life and to make this available to the supplier or his designers. This type of information is important when replacement decisions have to be made on a rational basis. The capabilities of a machine are best monitored, and certainly assisted, by periodical checks on its products or work, to ensure that the performance of the machine has not fallen below a tolerable level.

Machines occasionally break down even under the most benign conditions of operation. To mitigate any possible serious effect on production, consideration may have to be given to the availability of stand-by equipment. The cost of this duplication (or multiplication) may appear high, but can still be justifiable by the advantages of virtually uninterrupted production which would otherwise be lost because of a breakdown or even the need for routine attention. Stand-by policy can be adopted in simpler ways, such as by the use of "flexible" machines, capable of being used in more than one way (although fundamentally a design for a particular purpose is usually better), or sometimes by duplication of vulnerable components in the actual design.

The need for readily available spares is an obvious one, but where a spare is in the nature of an insurance item—that is, where it is hoped never to have to use it, but if required it is of vital importance—justification for holding unmoving stock may have to be undertaken.

Material. As soon as material comes into a department, it is the manager's responsibility. Material can be widely defined as anything on which some work has to be performed, so it can vary from raw material such as chemicals, rubber, and steel to sub-assemblies such as gear-boxes. The material has to come in at the right time and in the right quantity and quality. The manager is responsible for ensuring that he wastes no time on faulty material by initiating the necessary steps to be taken. These include inspection or the requirement of quality certification or labelling, suitably checked periodically. He must also involve any necessary assistance to make sure that material arrives into his department at the right rate and time.

Quality procedures may result in delay between arrival of material into his department and putting it into process. In that case, it may be advisable to have a "no man's land" or "quarantine" into which unchecked (by his department) material can be placed and from which, only after verification, suitable material can be drawn. The checking, identification and/or labelling of material as suitable, while being the manager's responsibility, need not necessarily be done by him or his representative. It is quite usual to involve technologists or technically trained personnel who may be responsible to a technical department.

Whatever the procedure, however, it must be so completely watertight, simple, and unambiguous that there is no possibility whatever for process work or manufacture to proceed with other than certified correct material. If labels are used for certification, colours may not be sufficiently distinguishable in cases of partial colour blindness; so colours ought to be allied to other distinguishing features such as shape. It is also axiomatic that, following certification, all necessary precautions must be taken to preclude the possibility of change or deterioration—for example, by the introduction of foreign matter or dirt.

Allied with the checking of suitability and labelling, there must be a procedure for the handling of unsuitable material. This must also be clearly identified in such a way as to prevent the possibility of its use not only then, but also at some later time (unless adjusted, in which case it should be treated as newly incoming). There must be no doubt as to its true quality even if removed for other uses. All identification attached, and which might indicate what it purported to be, must be removed and only the true facts left.

Physical characteristics of people

Besides departmental responsibilities in relation to the organisation of men, machines, and material, it is important for managers to know the quantified physical capabilities of each. Much has been written about machines, especially in relation to the statistical aspects of quality control. The necessity for ensuring machine capability to achieve continuing compliance with the requirements and the importance of maintaining the calibration of instruments, are all part of this. In these contexts, however, not enough has been said about the human machine, although there are some available data from such studies as anthropometry. The provision of good working conditions and amenities has tended to be considered from purely sociological aspects, the effects looked at hopefully from the qualitative rather than the quantitative point of view. It is true that the operator has much less influence on quality, or lack of it, than is often supposed. In fact, it has been confirmed independently in both the United Kingdom and the United States [F Nixon, Services/Industry Conference, London, February 1968] that the responsibility for manufacturing and quality defects rests on management and operators roughly in the proportion 4:1. That is, the deficiencies and inadequacies in design, and particularly in planning and training, have a far greater effect on quality than an operator's personal inefficiency.

Nevertheless, it is necessary for management to take positive action in relating equipment to the men who use it, and in optimising the environmental and social conditions in which they work. Conversely, men have to be related to the equipment and tasks, not only by the necessary training and instruction which are, of course, of paramount importance, but also, to as great an extent as possible, by physical qualities and temperament.

The uniform, or, at least, reasonably predictable working of human beings can be a matter of special concern in some circumstances, and it may be necessary to take into account their "personal equations." This applies especially to observers and inspectors. Colour blindness is not an uncommon defect in males, yet how many personnel managers make this a feature of examination in choosing say, an electrician, to whom the unmistakeable distinction between red and green is usually vital for safety? Defective sight can give rise to the wrong measurement of angles, and variations in the rapidity of nervous action can lead to errors in timing.

The possible serious consequences, commercially, of the effect of the latter came to the author's attention during the instruction of National Coal Board inspectors in the procedures for a fire-resistance test. One of the specified tests involved a criterion of a maximum of three seconds between the removal of a burner, with standard flame, from the specimen, and complete extinction of flame in the specimen. The test involved starting and stopping a stop-watch from visual signals, the first of which was controllable and could be anticipated, and the second of which was a matter of subjective opinion. A considerable quantity of the commodity in question could be rejected as a result of recording a mean value (over six tests) of, say 3.1 seconds. Although the average total error over each timing would be reduced over six timings (theoretically in the proportion $\sqrt{6}:1$, according to the laws of accidental error), it became obvious that poor vision or slow nervous response in an inspector could produce embarrassment between manufacturer and purchaser.

In appointing any test personnel or inspectors who might be involved in timing, it is therefore necessary to make simple examinations or checks to ensure that there is no unacceptably large personal error. These might merely be the starting and immediate stopping of a three-action stop-watch (start, stop, return) at a given signal, the watch recording an interval related to the rate of response. That this type of precaution may be necessary can be illustrated by many examples, of which the first recorded may have been in 1796 when Maskelyne, the Astronomer Royal, having accused an assistant of inattention and carelessness resulting in persistent lateness is making certain recordings, dismissed him. Considerable interest was aroused and it was later proved that the assistant was not lacking in care and attention, but that his personal qualities included constitutional slowness in response. In the author's own experience, there is a certain first-class honours graduate in engineering whose response to a signal in his university days was as slow as 0.8 seconds (the normal value rarely exceeding half this). This feature of his personality was not, however, taken into account when providing him with a driving licence.

If the inspection or measurement of, or merely the looking at, angles is involved in any operation, it would certainly be a matter of prudence to find out whether the man concerned suffered from some degree of astigmatism in his eyes—a not uncommon defect.

The emergence of a systematic quality defect often results in a complex series of costly investigations involving the interruption of production, or the rearrangement of production by switching machines or operators, in order to attempt to isolate the source of defect. Precautions such as those indicated above are usually simple to take and often preclude the necessity for making these investigations.

Having taken steps towards choosing the right man for a particular job, it still has to be recognised that the human machine has a limited range of capabilities. It may be necessary to adjust the job, the equipment, or the specification to the man. If, in the above example of timings, 10.1 second is of critical importance and if, by and large, the speed of nervous response of most men is of the same magnitude or larger, than it has to be considered whether:

1   The requirement is so critical that it *must* be met.
2   The requirement is such that certain relaxations can be made to suit the operator.

In the first case, it may be necessary to devise other means of measurement or to eliminate the human machine from the measurement. In the second, the specification may require examination for possible modification, or the method of applying the criterion adjusted. For instance, the stipulation of a maximum of 3 seconds in the above example could be accompanied by instructions that the results need only be *recorded* to the nearest (say) half second and that they be expressed using fractions and not the decimal equivalents. Thus 3.1 could be recorded as 3 seconds and 3.3 as $3\frac{1}{2}$ seconds. The magnitude of these allowances in recording, should be carefully designed to mask the variations possible between one operator, or observer, and another. The method of expression should be designed to give a "feel" of the justifiable accuracy. A sensible procedure of this nature, wherever possible of course, can eliminate the possibilities of critical commercial effects being dependent on the normal physical differences experienced between men.

While it is more common among good management to consider the limitations of machines and so relate designs and specifications to these limitations, it is less often considered that the same type of consideration may be necessary in the case of the human machine.

Industrial motivations

Modern production methods, being designed to provide low specific costs, tend to break up the whole process into a number of relatively simple steps, each one of which is such a small part of the whole that operators become divorced from the finished product. In most industries or trades, therefore, relatively few people are able to interest themselves in following a product from design to final assembly. Thus the majority of workers lack the incentive of satisfaction in the ultimate products to which they are contributing some skill.

The criteria of success are not only functions of pure output or mass flow, nor even of "efficiency" in production—usually interpreted in terms of costs. They must also include the value of the goods produced in terms of a contribution to the achievement of the purpose for which they are intended; in other words the quality and reliability of the products are also important incentive elements. The industrial techniques which involve the operators in the processes of achieving these, in monitoring their own performance towards quality, and in assessing their own results, are also incentives which, in turn, increase their own effectiveness. So the problems to be tackled are not only those which result in higher output and lower costs, but also in compliance with the quality requirements. (In fact the first two can be attained without increase of mass flow, if the *proportion* of products of the required quality in the total output can be increased.)

A great deal of attention has been devoted to the techniques of production and quality control; less, unfortunately, has been paid to actual people. Yet the techniques have to be operated by people and, if their co-operation is first cultivated, the application of the techniques will follow quite easily; if their co-operation is not sought or assured, it becomes dubious whether any techniques will have a significant effect on the quality of the products.

It is not easy to ensure co-operation; still less to define the steps by which it can be achieved. It depends on personalities and management attitudes, and the general atmosphere pervading all levels of personnel. It is accompanied by pride in the job, and encouraged when the skill and ideas of management have been exercised properly and in accordance with the particular jobs. A craftsman or a designer may find this easier than an operator performing a monotonous production task, but even the latter can be helped by appropriate training and by keeping him constantly aware of the importance of his contribution to the success of the efforts of the team of which he is a member. Examination of all routine jobs should be made in order to attempt to increase the degree of skill involved; in this, the operator can often be consulted since he may have constructive ideas, which have been partially destroyed by the lack of interest in a monotonous, repetitive task.

The relation of the man to his job is important for other reasons, since a satisfactory solution may not only improve productivity in a direct way, but also in other ways such as by reducing carelessness arising from disinterest, improving absenteeism records, and lowering the accident rates.

The motivations which actuate workers vary in importance and degree of significance from company to company, industry to industry and, particularly, from nation to nation. They include money, job satisfaction, personal recognition, self-improvement, contribution to the company, contribution to the industry, and contribution to the national good. Particular care must be exercised in attempting to transfer the motivations of, say, our country to another. Money may be the most important factor in one, while personal recognition (even one's signature at the foot of a tennis club notice on a notice board) may be the greatest motivation in another country. As for contribution to the company, it is well known that in some companies, but more especially in others, the sense of belonging to, and being protected within, a family of which the benevolent father figure is the managing director, is a very strong motivation.

All these and any other motivations must be examined carefully, possibly in the light of order of importance, and then applied or encouraged accordingly.

Automation

While the introduction of automatic methods of production is a means of reducing specific costs, increasing output, and preserving uniformity of quality, it should be remembered that this type of equipment or system is incapable of judgement and can only operate on its "settings" or the instructions fed in. Therefore, it is necessary to take great precautions to ensure that the full requirements are put into the system, since there is much less opportunity to introduce the element of skill which otherwise could affect quality. Additionally, since the output rate is usually increased, it is more than ever necessary to monitor the capability of the system of continuing to produce a compliant product. Automation transfers the control by the worker from a machine or part of the system to the process itself. This is a wider responsibility and may be much more exacting although the activities are of greater significance. Human capabilities, therefore, must not be stretched or exceeded by the demands of the system, and the introduction of such means of production should not reduce the relation of the worker to his job. These considerations require intelligent management, the efficient use of ergonomic studies, and the provision of the proper incentives, which include not only the prospects of financial reward, or the fear of dismissal, but also the involvement and interest of the worker in the whole process.

Workers and standards

Mention is made in Chapter 4 of methods of monitoring performance by pure mass flow. Unfortunately, the earnings of workers are too often geared, by some payment-by-results formula, to output. This is, of course, not necessarily the same as productivity. It might be perfectly understandable to a worker if his rewards were to be measured as a function of good work only, provided that:

1   The goodness of his work is accurately defined so that he knows exactly what is required.
2   He can, wherever possible, assess his work in relation to goodness.

The first requires a standard or specification which, if properly constructed, means exactly the same thing to worker, supervisor, inspector, or anyone at all involved in that particular work and prevents disagreements as to what is right and what is wrong or what quality is required. Opinions are eliminated. If it is not possible to produce a specification (or, of course, the relevant clauses), it may still be necessary to standardise the requirement in another form. Workers rarely claim that standards are too rigorous; usually their complaint is that they are too vague or insufficiently clearly defined. As an example of a standard requirement, a component of a pressurised system would be specified not only by its dimensional characteristics, but also by the property that it has to withstand a given pneumatic pressure in operation. Other parts of the whole specification—for example, materials—would be irrelevant to the worker and beyond his control. The appropriate drawing(s) and values, in bold presentation, would be prominently displayed in front of him in a form incapable of misinterpretation.

The level of quality of a product may not be the highest, but the optimum arrived at by all the external factors, most particularly the customer's exact needs (especially in regard to the price he is prepared to pay). This must be explained to the worker in terms of making his work most effective. He will understand that for most purposes it is not necessary to have the highest quality; he will certainly accept that making a product dearer than necessary will affect its chances of being sold, and his own continuing prosperity.

The second proviso requires that whenever possible the worker should be his own judge of quality output, his own inspector. In some cases this can be done simply by comparison with a standard, which may even be a picture of what is good and what is bad. In other cases it may be necessary to add to his training sufficient information for him to make the appropriate measurements or readings, or to take samples. In any case, he should be able to appreciate the significance and import-ance of any monitoring data, quality control charts, or avoidable waste figures, which are at hand, and their relation to his degree of success. This is one particularly important way of increasing his interest and exercising more skill. Using the previous example, inspection can be performed by the use of suitable gauges (non-measuring) fixed in a convenient manner and capable of being used easily and quickly. The component can be applied to one or more of these to prove its dimen-sions. "Go" and "no-go" features would insure that critical tolerances were satisfactory. Where the criterion involves assembly with another component made elsewhere, the gauges can, with advantage, be exact models of the permissible extremes of the latter.

Having passed the dimensional requirements, the component can be fitted to a simple and convenient test, often simulating its ultimate assembly, to which compressed air can be applied. The criterion here should be simply a coloured sector on a (periodically calibrated) pressure gauge—equivalent to the desired pressure limits.

As with dimensional tests, the worker is not expected to *measure* any property, and the actual figures on the gauge are of secondary import-ance to him. The important features of monitoring performance are speed, ease, convenience, and simple criteria.

Where a worker's performance can only be measured by someone else—for example by an inspector—it is advisable to ensure close communication between the two so that the necessary information is known to the worker. Any situation, in which he is unaware of his achievement must be avoided.

Four

Increasing the Proportion of Good Quality

Departmental management has little immediate influence on Q and R values. These have usually been built in to the product at design, development, and specification stages. Nevertheless, it is their responsibility, not the inspectors', to ensure that procedures and processes under their control are capable of producing compliant articles. There are ways, however, in which management activities have a long-term influence on Q and R. These vary from one company to another, but one is to examine products in "product groups" including wide representation. Under the chairmanship of a departmental manager, there might be a designer, production engineer, inspector or quality engineer, an operator—plus any necessary specialists.

Product examination

The product is examined from the different points of view. High on the agenda of meetings of the group are examinations of Q and R data (particularly complaints from any source) to find solutions to any troubles revealed. One large organisation found that such a group gradually arrived at formal studies of product performance and reliability. They were periodically allowed to drop normal duties for a short time and, helped by lectures and discussions on reliability, produced proposals for the board to convert into a programme of action. This was allied to a time schedule so that reviews of results could be made periodically.

The basis for the work was mainly information fed back from sub-contractors, users, purchasers, and storekeepers, which included usage complaints, rates of movement of spares, and frequency of maintenance.

As a result of this type of examination it will be found that the intrinsic reliability of a product—that is, that value built in by care taken in design, testing, and production—can be increased substantially.

A system for product examination is always necessary where increase in reliability is sought and, whether it is on the above lines or not, should generally follow stages such as the following:

1 *Educate for reliability.* The group concerned must be made fully aware of the importance of basics such as the control of quality, the performance required, the reasonable expectation of life, and the factors of environment and variations of use. They must review their own stages of design, etc, in the light of these, as well as the possible behaviour of users.

2 *Identify trouble.* Identify trouble or deficiencies of product by examination of information from all sources.

Failed or inadequate products must be sought out for exhaustive technical examination by specialists. Complaints can be analysed. Difficulties experienced in production, packing, storage, transport, or installation should also be collected.

3 *Establish reasons.* The technical examinations and the various analyses produce the facts. Now these have to be considered for possible causes of failure or inadequacy. Judgement has to be used.

4 *Attempt to reproduce trouble and, if possible, life pattern, by testing.* The tests set up should be based on the reasons assumed— for example, for failure. They will then show whether the previous judgement is right or not. If it is convenient to test to the end of the life of a product, this can provide evidence as to causes of trouble. Sometimes accelerated tests, by overload, overspeed, or increase of abuse, can produce a pattern of failure similar to that experienced.

5 *Re-educate for reliability as necessary.* If by now the various unreliabilities and the causes have been identified, it may be necessary to educate for specific techniques of removing particular kinds of unreliability. For example, there are special methods of designing tests which will give the maximum information leading to performance improvement. Fatigue failures may require examination of the possible effects of this phenomenon and its wide variation in common design materials.

6 *Modify product to remove deficiencies.* This is the actual stage of increasing reliability by reducing unreliabilities. If the previous steps have pointed to and confirmed a weak spot and its causes, the designers now go ahead to adjust the design, improve the part, or strengthen a member. Sometimes a major alteration may be necessary by virtue of the consequential effects set in train by the change in one part.

7 *Take all necessary parallel steps.* For example, adjust specification, inform inspection. It is normally unwise to make an immediate change to a specification until a fair amount of experience of the modification has been gained from use. It is necessary, however, to issue amendment slips or similar papers to those concerned with working to the specification. These include operators, inspectors, sub-contractors, and quality personnel.

8 *Check effectiveness of action by repeat testing.* The same routine of testing that was set up for 4 above should be applied in order to evaluate the actions in removing unreliabilities. Failures should have been removed (or deferred); life should be extended.

9 *Adjust into production.* Any changes in processing which become necessary as a result of the design modifications have now to be made to the production line, concurrently making consequential adjustments to the controls which will ensure the new requirements being met.

10 *Audit by re-examination of sources for those or any other troubles.* Obviously the changes have been made for the purpose of eliminating or reducing particular troubles. The same organisation which produced the information for 2 must carry on (reliability improvement is a continuing process), and produce data which measure the success or otherwise of the steps taken for particular purposes. This process often reveals new troubles, either as a direct result of the changes made or which were masked in importance by the original ones. The whole procedure in all its stages, carries on and deals with these.

45

11 *Finalise and seal successful actions.* A design modification which, as a result of test experience 8 and feed back from usage 10 is clearly an improvement, should now be completely formalised into specification, drawings, instructions, etc, and made known to all concerned (who should acknowledge receipt of any such information). Advertising, sales, and public relations may be involved here with advantage.

A permanent set-up based on the above lines, even though occupying its participants for a relatively small proportion of their working time, *cannot fail* to make continual improvement.

Monitoring Performance

Mass flow or pure output measurement. Many systems of measurement of production performance rely on mass flow or its equivalent—that is throughput of weight, area, volume, and numbers etc. The flow is complicated by the effects of work in actual progress and by work in stock, by the different rates at which parts of an assembly arrive at the actual assembling point, and so on. In general, the systems are pipelines and this analogy is often used colloquially.

Where the systems are fairly complex, the optimum flow can be arrived at by the use of critical path techniques which, in effect, represent them as pipeline systems and quantify each part of them in terms of flow rate, etc. [*See* for example: A Battersby, *Network Analysis for Planning and Scheduling*, Macmillan.] Allowances can be made for parts of processes in series—that is, one following another—or in parallel—that is, proceeding at the same time if not at the same rate. Stock can be simulated by the presence of a collecting point or "capacity" in the line whose magnitude is determined by the sporadic requirement to increase the outflow suddenly to a certain level and for a given duration. On the other hand, it may be sufficiently important to use stock to maintain the outflow at a given level even when some previous part of the system is throttled by failure of equipment or supply. In these ways customer demand can be satisfied even when it fluctuates—always assuming it is profitable to do so.

All systems of mass flow must be reviewed constantly and carefully in the light of profitability; noting that no profit is earned until the goods have been delivered and the customer has been satisfied. The parameters observed in these systems can only be considered as intermediate pointers to profitability by way of the conformance of production flow to the original intentions or plan. They should not be included in any performance-by-profit system.

Nevertheless, it is immediately obvious that the principle features of mass flow monitoring, besides volumetric rate of flow, also include the facility to control the conservation of material (mass). For, over reasonable periods, what goes in must come out—albeit in a different form: weight in, equals weight out. Making appropriate corrections for any accumulations, or otherwise, in the processing stages or in reservoir or storage stages, the total amount of material flowing in has to be equated to that emerging as products plus waste. In this way the possible loss of material for any reason can be kept under scrutiny, as can the proportion of waste.

Reworked material can also be monitored using rate of mass flow as a criterion, the correct analogy being a local recirculation in the pipe-line—or an apparent increase in resistance to, and reduction in, flow rate in one particular area. Sporadic increases in production costs can thus be quantified. Waste quantities are usually separated into two classes—those which are unavoidable and those which are avoidable.

Unavoidable waste. The first category can be illustrated by an elementary example of the requirement to stamp out circular blanks from a sheet of material. Theoretically, the greatest economy would be that arrangement in which the circles touched each other and had centres at the corners of equilateral triangles. For practical reasons, it may not be possible to achieve this low value of unavoidable waste. To obtain clean cut edges or to keep the waste in one coherent piece, the circular blanks may have to be separated by a margin. In that case the unavoidable waste would be greater. Figure 4 shows the situation in which the area of sheet is assumed sufficiently large to ignore edge effects. The equilateral triangle is typical of the whole area and calculation of waste can be made from it. The unavoidable waste is the area of the triangle, less one-half (three-sixths) of the area of a circle.

If d is the diameter of the blank and t the distance between blanks, for different values of $\dfrac{t}{d}$ this gives:

$\dfrac{t}{d}$	0	0.15	0.1	0.2	0.3
UW	9.3	17.7	25.0	37.0	46.3%

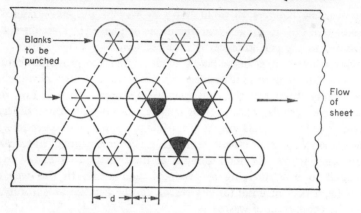

FIGURE 4   PROPORTION OF UNAVOIDABLE WASTE
The punching of circular blanks from a sheet is a simple
example of how a fixed proportion of unavoidable waste is
built in at the design stage.

This shows the vast effect of the margin on the proportion of original
material remaining as unavoidable waste, and the reason for its being
kept as low as possible.

Unavoidable waste is only unavoidable because the design of product,
nature of raw materials, and method of production have been fixed.
It can sometimes be reduced by attention at the design stage, and
by procedures which form part of value engineering examinations. By
its nature it is rarely the responsibility of production personnel.

Avoidable waste. On the other hand, the second category, avoidable
waste, which needs no explanation, has normally no *direct* connection
with design stages, and so on, and is usually controllable by production personnel. (There are sometimes indirect connections with design
or methods of production which lend themselves to peculiar difficulties
of manufacture.) For that reason quantitative information about
avoidable waste must always and continuously be immediately available
to production personnel, and in particular, to operators. Avoidable
waste competitions, at any level, in which each operator (or each
department) sees an actual picture of his (its) own continuing performance are as salutary in creating the right atmosphere to produce
improvement as the presence of a "policeman" for supervisory reasons.

In what follows, the term "avoidable waste" may be referred to as
including not only waste in the sense of unused or unusable material,

but also waste of resources, waste involved in not achieving requisite qualities, and so on. It is an important factor in the cost of unreliability of production and involved with "unreliability" or "defects" in their widest sense.

The units in which avoidable waste can be measured should vary according to the circumstances. In some cases it is quite sufficient to monitor by the direct units of the mass flow—that is, weight, volume, area, length, numbers, and so on; in others by equivalent loss of saleable value or even profit. This second procedure of using a monetary value may be much more revealing than mere units of output.

Having set up a system in which the waste performance is instantly available to all concerned, it is sometimes augmented by the fixing of a target figure which it is hoped to attain. Great care and thought must be given to this since it may not provide the atmosphere of improvement or development intended. Sometimes the target can be attained in a short time and this either results in complacency about that level or scepticism when it is altered too frequently. Sometimes it is so unattainable in a reasonable time that it creates a mild form of indifference, or can even be disheartening. Therefore, it may be good policy to rely on natural efforts to achieve a steady and general improvement rather than to fix a target. Better still would be to set up some competitive atmosphere if possible.

When actual competitions are set up between departments, the points to be taken into account are:

1   The relative differences in degrees of difficulty and levels of waste performance.
2   The law of diminishing returns—that is, the fact that it is less easy to improve if the performance is already high.

These considerations necessitate the devising of fair methods of comparison and perhaps the setting up of individual norms and targets on some rational basis.

Production performance on a profit basis. Quantitative monitoring of performance by any method at all, is an instrument by means of which management always arrives at a justification for the introduction of activities which lie within the scope of quality and reliability. Waste, avoidable or unavoidable, is a part of the cost of unreliability, and continuous measurement of production leads to steps to improve efficiency in the sense of degree of goodness. However, since the object is to maximise profit, the best method of monitoring is that which measures performance in terms of profit rather than throughout. Managers have to be profit-conscious in any case, but this attitude has to be refined by actual quantification, so that at the same time as the mass flow is measured for the necessary reasons referred to above, the output should be converted to profit measurement.

This can be done in many ways and is sometimes beset with complications, some of which are mentioned later. For the purposes of illustration, let us consider the simple case of a department manufacturing a number of products in an unchanging and continuous stream. Examination of the overall costs and returns that are normally made elsewhere will have produced figures for the relative profitabilities of each of the products. Without necessarily using these actual profit figures, a profit index (PI), directly proportional to the profit, can be allocated to each product. These indices should preferably be simple integers to speed examination and to minimise possibilities of error. However the output is measured in the mass flow monitoring, the individual product quantities should be multiplied by the corresponding indices in a further column of the table of production data. This is labelled "profit performance" (PP). The total values of the output or mass flow columns can then be confined to the analysis of waste, and the PP column used as a measure of the worth of a department's performance.

Figure 5 shows a highly simplified examination of hypothetical performances in two consecutive weeks. Had the examination been confined to output only, the mass flow totals show an increase of 1950 to 2150 units or about 10 per cent, which would appear to be a sate of improvement or one of self-satisfaction for the manager of the department. However, looking at the significant features, it can be seen that the profit has fallen from 3600 to 2950 units, a drop of about 18 per cent, a source for less satisfaction. The profit indices are, as indicated above, merely relative values, the figures relating to absolute profit only, and, therefore, being independent of the cost or selling price of the different products. For example, product A may be selling at 100 shillings (£5) a square metre with a profit of one shilling (£0.05) while product D may be selling at 30 shillings (£1.50) a square metre with a profit of 10 shillings (£0.50).

Obviously PIs must be kept under close review and constantly brought up to date. The complications which can make this type of monitoring less easy than indicated in the example are, of course,

Week 12			
Product	Output (sq yd)	Profit index	Profit performance
A	1000	1	1000
B	600	2	1200
C	300	3	900
D	50	10	500
Totals	1950		3600

Week 13			
Product	Output (sq yd)	Profit index	Profit performance
A	1500	1	1500
B	500	2	1000
C	150	3	450
D	—	10	—
Totals	2150		2950

FIGURE 5   PROFIT PERFORMANCE

An increase in output is not necessarily an increase in profit.

many and varied. They include the possibility of more than one selling price for one product, as for instance when different quantities or different customers are involved. Changes in rates of production or usage of equipment, the demands of extra shifts or for overtime charges, can affect the analysis. The costs of materials and other direct influences on profit must be carefully watched.

Mention was made of stable and continuous production, and therefore periods of development or output to test marketability require special attention. In this last case, for profit some other desirability can be substituted and the return for investment measured in terms of other rewards. The important thing is to ensure that the system is carefully tailor-made to match the procedures and circumstances.

Since profit is only achieved by selling, production for stock has to be considered in terms of notional profit, for, presumably, the particular stock level is only maintained to maximise the rate of sales. This is particularly important since it may be necessary to allot priorities in production for stock; the departmental performance must not be affected adversely as a result of these priorities.

It is clear that this type of monitoring is aimed especially at departments which produce more than one product. It can, of course, be used to compare the performances of smaller units than departments—namely sections or even single machines.

The effects of introducing this type of system, making any necessary allowances in the case of complications referred to above, can be quite far reaching. Using straight-forward output figures as a measure of performance, there is no guarantee that the more profitable products receive the priority attention that they ought to have. It is often the case that the products receiving priority are those which require least effort, trouble, and attention, to produce the greatest contributions to the mass output and apparent performance. By their very nature they are usually (not always) the low profit ones, such as product A in the example.

Monitoring performance on a profit basis tends to orientate the priorities towards the higher profit products, which are therefore dealt with first. In turn, this has repercussions throughout the organisation, in that delivery promises or quotations tend to be adjusted correspondingly. Low profitability items, now put back in priority of production, are associated with longer delivery times, higher profit items with shorter delivery times—which has an intrinsic benefit, and also gains further custom. One further bonus in this procedure of weighting performance by PI is the accumulation of experience and awareness of what actually makes profit in a product. This provides an excellent and fruitful atmosphere for development.

Isolation and elimination of defects

The achievement of quality requires the application of techniques, some of which are of the most refined type, that involve statistical methods. All these, incidentally, must be considered as parts of the production processes—which should be aimed at producing good output, not merely output. Before introducing these techniques, however, it is necessary to observe that the overwhelming contribution to quality is made by activities which can be classified as, simply, good housekeeping. Most of these require no quantification—they involve cleanliness and working in good light, and so on—but having established this "atmosphere" it is then necessary for all concerned to know what is being done correctly.

If specifications are to be complied with, or any stipulations to be met, the relevant information required should be displayed prominently at the work point. The results of tests or checks against these requirements are recorded continuously and also put up near the specification display. In this connection, it is neccessary to consider that least effort, in assimilation of this type of information, is required by pictorial rather than tabular information. The object is to recognise trends and to prevent, rather than cure, anything which threatens saleability.

Production reliability, as with the reliability of design, is always best tackled in the negative sense by the isolation of, and then the reduction in, unreliabilities. The display of what may be a trend towards their increase, is the first step leading to corrective action, which is then visually justified by a reversal of the trend. The corrective action is the elimination of defects in the processing, which result in what may be generally termed avoidable waste.

Attitude to a tolerable level of defects. The quantification and display of defect levels is the complement of that of good output and can be used to magnify the shortcomings of the latter. It can be a powerful help in reduction of unreliability, but it may be necessary to overcome certain fixed mental attitudes of operators and lower management to levels of waste. It is often found that there exists a sense or feeling that a specific level is tolerable; as long as the scrap doesn't exceed 5 per cent, everything is considered to be normal. This attitude is responsible for eating heavily into possible profits and should be vigorously fought. Of course, should the defect level rise suddenly to 15 per cent for any reason—accident, carelessness, negligence, failure, or whatever—urgent measures would be brought to bear, whether as a result of pressure from above or not. These might include investigation and correction to bring the situation back to "normal"—that is, 5 per cent scrap. The same measures, however, if related to the overall procedure of continuous defect or waste monitoring, could, in an atmosphere in which no level of waste were taken for granted, result in a downward trend. These measures should be outlined to those concerned in waste competitions.

Relative severity of defects. Before making decisions about steps to reduce the incidence of defects, their severity in terms of magnitude or frequency are obviously important. That type which recurs frequently may require and justify the expenditure of money and time to eradicate it: the type which occurs infrequently may best be dealt with by other methods—for example, by discarding and/or replacement. So in addition to monitoring defects (or waste) in the aggregate, it is necessary to include some means of weighting individual items for severity. These may be by any reasonable criterion such as loss of material, time, or money. Records must be kept by each department—and periodical statements issued to those concerned, including, where necessary, other involved departments.

In accordance with the requirement to operate as efficiently as possible, all monitoring and associated paper work must not only be kept to a minimum in total volume, but also be so designed to provide only the basic information required, no more and no less. There is always an inherent dislike of paper work; it appears to be divorced from the production processes and it is a nuisance. For this reason, it is far better to arrange it so that no essays or opinions are sought, merely "yes" or "no," a tick or a cross, where possible. In its formulation stages, careful thought has to be given as to what is really wanted.

In the case of defect severity, the first information required is certainly not great detail of the actual nature or the cause of the defect. For if that particular defect happened on an isolated occasion, had never happened before, and might not reasonably be expected ever to happen again, it would clearly be a waste of time and money to examine it in detail. Where the nature of the organisation is such that defects or failures information is collected from many sources for examination at a central point, this is extremely important. The information first required should then be identification, location in space and time, and severity in magnitude. An analysis of this type of information which, of course, has to be designed to suit the circumstances, and which is usually a matter of nothing more than simple addition, should show overall severity and source (not necessarily cause) of defect.

Overall severity. Taking this first, the analysis shows immediately whether it is worth proceeding further or not. If the defect magnitude is small (in the chosen terms of time or money lost), and if it is infrequent, it would be an additional waste of time and money even to read further. This is why it may not be advisable to design the recording medium to provide information that is too comprehensive. On the other hand, for some of those defects which appear to be of sufficient severity in magnitude or frequency (the latter being more important), additional information may be necessary. This could be easy, and derived from further examination of the records, or it might require an investigation.

Source. A simple examination of a defect of adequate severity to justify action, can show whether or not it is random in source. It may, for instance, be scattered among operators, machines, sections, departments, or even factories in a large organisation. Investigational and corrective action taken at one point is likely to be applicable universally. On the other hand, the arithmetical evidence may clearly point to a relationship with one or more of these areas. In this case, the first approach must be to make transpositions—for example, switching operators or machines to attempt to confirm this diagnosis and to pinpoint the source before seeking cause. Well-designed procedures, after the manner of operational research, can produce quite interesting information. Such things can emerge as the effects of bad light, dirty atmosphere, carelessness, or insufficiency of training, the deterioration in performance of machines or, most often, peculiar local difficulties. Again, to have had information too detailed might have been superfluous before the source had been identified.

Where a formal defects scheme is in operation in a large user organisation, it is sometimes thought necessary to by-pass it locally in order to resolve an urgent difficulty. A direct approach to the supplier might elicit the information that the defect in question was unique (whether it was or not). However, the same trouble or defect may have been repeated elsewhere many times. Isolated by itself, it appears to be the interest only of local users and the supplier could well convince them that it was indeed an isolated fault. If, however, it is or has been experienced elsewhere in the organisation it is important, in the interests of increase in reliability, to collect the overall information, which will show whether the defect is due to inadequacy of the equipment, or the local installation and use, or difficult local conditions. The remedy may be redesign rather than single replacement.

	Defects record			Period 16
Defect	Reasons (if known)	Total time lost (min)	% of total	Cumulative %
1 Low strength	Raw material quality	1030	24·2	24·2
2 Weld fracture	Contamination	820	19·3	43·5
3 Poor fit	Tolerances?	680	16·0	59·5
21 (: : : :)	(: : : :)	4	0·1	100·0
	Totals	4250	100·0	

FIGURE 6   THE VITAL FEW DEFECTS
In this case the first three defects account for nearly 60 per cent of the total. Action should be concentrated on these.

Vital few defects. When, as is usually the case, there are a number of sources of waste, unreliability, or defects which might require action, a decision has to be made as to the allocation of limited resources to this action. The previous type of recording will have thrown up those in this category and thrown out those on which it is proposed not to proceed further. The severity of these should now be listed in actual order of magnitude as is shown in Figure 6 which must be exhibited in the department as well as circulated where necessary. The first column numbers and names the defect; the second gives cause if known, but may not be essential primarily. The next column is the severity in terms of loss of time or money, deliberately arranged in order of magnitude, and this is totalled to give the aggregate loss in the period indicated. The fourth column shows the proportion of the total loss incurred by each defect; and the last column gives a running or cumulative total. In the example shown it will be seen that there were apparently twenty-one types of defects of which the first three alone accounted for nearly 60 per cent of the total loss. This is quite a usual situation.

The resources available can now be profitably applied to the reduction or elimination of the losses corresponding to, say, the first three defects—the vital few. The focussing of attention on these by all concerned is the important step.

Investigations and corrective action are confined to these alone and it can usually be seen where efforts must be concentrated—in a preliminary stage such as incoming material quality, or pre-processing adequacy, or in some departmental activity. This continuing process will keep showing that a few troubles account for more than half of all troubles, and as correction takes place, those at the top will change. The success of the actions will be measured by generally continuing reduction in the total loss and consequential improvement in productivity.

Five

Standardisation and Specification

Before discussing this subject it is necessary to clarify the difference between "standard" and "specification" (and other parts of these words) which seems to cause confusion. It is not unusual to find one or other word used indiscriminately to mean the same thing; while this is justifiable in some cases it is certainly not in others. On occasion, the two words are used together and reference is made to a standard specification.

Implications of the two words

Dictionary definitions tend to give the right implications such as:

1   "To standardise"—to establish a rule, to make regular.
2   "To specify"—to prepare a detailed statement of particulars.

From these it can be sensed that standardisation is the action taken to regularise a practice, or as a result of a policy decision to standardise or pin something down or rationalise. Specification is much narrower and means simply an accurate stipulation of detailed characteristics and other requirements. Thus one can standardise on a complete specification, or alternatively, on a part of a specification or on a number of specifications. In the first case the specification can be called a (particular) standard, but in the second it cannot.

One can, of course, standardise without using a specification, such as on a practice, a convention, or a procedure rather than a tangible thing, but it will always be found to be necessary to prescribe—that is, specify—in some way what is required. Hence, a specification is an instrument of standardisation and provides the opportunity for saying "this is what is required in the standard practice, or this is the standard thing wanted." The specification document can, therefore, be accompanied or preceded by an order or command making its requirements mandatory or recommendatory as the case may be, as is discussed in a later section dealing with standardisation practice.

Examples. The following might help to illustrate the differences described above:

1   In one industry, a policy decision was taken to standardise on unified inch screw threads, working only to . . . (specification numbers).
2   The maximum speed for underground belt conveyors in British coal mines has been standardised at 500 feet (152. 4m) a minute.
3   The testing of all materials and equipment in organisation X shall be in accordance with British Standard Specifications wherever available.
4   To preclude the possibility of mistakes, it has been decided to use hexagonal nipples for greasing points, and circular nipples for oiling points.
5   The goods required shall be exactly in accordance with items number A, B, and D only in Clause 14 of Specification number X.
6   All mail shall be opened in the registry and stamped with the time and date of receipt.

Standards organisations

Organisations and departments which produce specifications are standardising bodies. These include the International Organisation for Standardisation (ISO); various national bodies such as the British Standards Institution (BSI), and corresponding bodies in other countries such as Association Francaise de Normalisation in France. Deutscher Normenausschuss in Germany; industry bodies such as the Society of Automotive Engineers (SAE) in the USA; and so on down to company level. The greater the "audience" for the ultimate specification, the longer it takes to prepare, since consultation obviously has to be wider and more comprehensive.

Specification

First approach in writing a specification. Before deciding to write a specification, it should first be ascertained whether there is already one in existence which is completely suitable or which may be easily adjusted to fulfil the required purpose. The best approach is to consult the national standards organisation, which not only maintains records of its own publications, but is also in intimate communication with other national bodies, international organisations (which, however, are not likely to have anything that is not available to national bodies), and a good part of industry. Should there be a completely adequate specification, it is only necessary to quote this in any standardisation activity, such as purchasing to that standard. Where there may be one that is not quite adequate, it is quoted together with details of the required variation, deletion, or addition. This type of procedure is far quicker and cheaper than starting from first principles.

Where no suitable specification exists it may be possible to approach the national body to prepare one. This will usually be agreed if there is a big enough potential use. However, the construction, the work of a committee of users and manufacturers plus specification experts, would take a long time. Therefore, when time is important, it is probably better to attempt to draw up the specification as a domestic document. Even in this case it is important to keep the national body apprised of what is going on (if not private and secret, of course), and to consider whether it might be possible to convert this document, at a much later stage, into one having wider use—for example, a national specification. Then, the first could, if necessary, be withdrawn in favour of the latter.

In all that follows, the use of the two words "standard" and "specification" (and other parts of the words) may be interchangeable in some places and not in others, but it is hoped that, in the light of the above examples, the context will make the meaning quite clear.

What is a specification? A specification is a document which accurately describes the requirements of one party, and which is therefore an excellent means of communicating those exact requirements to another. The requirements may be in the form of a purpose, performance, or duty with no reference to the means of achieving these, as when a prospective user wishes to seek the help of a designer to envisage the means of achievement. They may be in the form of details of a thing or machine, with no reference to how it is to be made, as when the designer communicates with the manufacturer, whose job it is to make it. They may be completely detailed bits and pieces, with dimensions, tolerances, materials, types of construction or manufacture, requirements of finish, and so on, and also methods of testing which enable all these requirements to be controlled and checked. This is when the manufacturer issues it, sectionalised as necessary, to those of his staff who are responsible for the actual production. They may be in the form of a description of the suitability for one or more purposes to satisfy either a known need or a potential need, as when a selling organisation approaches a prospective customer. The requirements may be descriptions of procedures, actions, or services as well as tangible things; they may, indeed, be some or all of the above in one document.

Under these circumstances, it can be seen that the contents and headings of a specification will vary according to the purpose for which it was written, and to the destination for which it is intended. The complexity of the document will also vary according to the numbers and types of requirements, although certain features are virtually common to all specifications.

Language of a specification. Although the word "specification" itself has a scientific or engineering flavour, and discussions such as those described above introduce terms such as manufacture, production, dimensions, and tests, a specification is not to be confined to these fields. Fortunately, the activities of consumer bodies in regard to common domestic articles and services, have shown the need to apply this type of thinking even to the most mundane areas. Therefore, it is necessary to adopt rational thinking and precise methods of expression which may have the flavour of technology. This is nothing new in a world that is slowly accepting these terminologies as a matter of course, chiefly necessitated by the introduction of technological equipment into the domestic sphere.

The requirements of a specification have to be described in accurate and unambiguous terms which necessitate a certain degree of proficiency with language, and a knowledge of the exact meaning of words and the shades of difference between those possibly used for similar purposes. To describe what is required of an internal combustion engine, or a vacuum cleaner, or a soap powder can all come under such a word as "performance" whose dictionary definition is clearly not related merely to engineering, although it appears to be. Where

61

possible, the language of a specification should be terse, with the use of the minimum number of words necessary to convey excactly what is intended. Figures and other values are much more precise than descriptions and can always be used to advantage; tables of these are particularly helpful and concise, especially where the units are carefully chosen.

Besides using simplified language, care must be taken to avoid expressions which are not quantifiable or which may be interpreted differently by different readers. To describe a requirement in terms such as "a smooth finish," "as clean as possible," "of sufficient strength," "in accordance with usual practice," etc, is not specifying and defeats the whole object of communicating unambiguous needs. One might as well call for as much compliance as possible.

Disadvantages of over-specifying. It is usual, in writing a specification, to describe a particular set of quality requirements which represent the best way of achieving the ultimate purpose. Thus, the quality should normally be optimum, not highest, and lead to the most economic fulfilment. It is well known that quality (and reliability) costs money, so it is unwise and extravagant to over-specify or to introduce requirements superfluous to, or beyond, those necessary to the particular intentions. Similarly, it is wasteful to call for values of properties higher than those really required. In addition to being unnecessarily costly, overspecifying in any of these forms is restrictive. It may preclude the possibility of obtaining adequate quality from a wider number of sources, automatically involve lengthier times of delivery, reduce the number of possible materials, and reduce the number of possible processes or means of manufacture.

In arriving at a specification, it is of the utmost importance to arrange communication and personal consultations between all the interested parties. These ensure that the ultimate document is indeed unambiguous and means the same thing to all. They are also necessary in order to arrive at mutual agreement to all the stipulations or, on the other hand, agreement to adjust or compromise for any reason.

Broad standardisation by the use of general specifications. Besides particular specifications describing discrete articles or services, a standardisation policy can be successfully based on general specifications. These usually deal with aspects of practice, details, or methods, which may be applicable not only to a number of similar machines, products, or services, but also to a very wide variety of these. For example, general specifications could be drawn up to refer to standards of design, workmanship, cleanliness, testing procedure, lubrication requirements, gears, and a host of other subjects which would be relevant throughout an organisation and which would not only *not* stultify design or initiative, but in fact, assist in these activities.

Development work, in particular, is speeded by the use of general specifications for units or procedures; in fact, it is very often an excellent plan to adopt some such standardisation policy actually during development. This sounds contradictory but, as is shown elsewhere (*see Chapter 7*) standardisation and development need not be incompatible. In this case, the general standardisation of certain features provides a feed of rationally based information from, for example, prototypes. This enables subsequent further standardisation, or may supply the necessary data for a specification otherwise difficult to construct.

NCQR/BSI Guide to the preparation of specifications

In 1965, the National Council for Quality and Reliability set up an *ad hoc* committee to consider the quality and reliability provisions in specifications. It was eventually agreed that other features could not be omitted and "the scope and practice of specification" appeared in the terms of reference. The committee, serviced by the BSI, did not consider the reasons leading to the requirement of a specification.

In May 1967, the *Guide to the Preparation of Specifications* was published by the BSI (PD 6112) with acknowledgement to the work of the NCQR.

At about the same time, interest in the same subject arose in meetings of the European Organisation for Quality Control, and a committee was set up to produce similar international guidance. In this case, the International Organisation for Standardisation was represented.

The main reason for examining the subject of specifying—a subject really the sphere of activity of standards organisations—was to apply expert knowledge to the inclusion of the appropriate provisions for quality and reliability.

The *Guide* is a mnemonic; it devotes itself less to telling the reader how to include the necessary clauses, than to remind him of those clauses. It gives headings of which only one main clause out of the seventeen is devoted to "characteristics," which is often thought to constitute the whole of a specification.

At the same time, it should be stressed that during its preparation, when literally thousands of comments were handled, much consideration was given to the importance of omitting certain features from the document, which were deemed to detract from its value. It was agreed that some of these would more properly be covered in accompanying contractual agreements. It is therefore important to examine the *Guide* as much for its omissions as for its contents. It does not clash with other publications on quality and reliability. For instance, it indicates that any method of defining reliability can be used, according to circumstances. Contemporaneous work on the reliability of, say, electronics components, fits this scheme of specification in a perfectly acceptable manner. In the *Guide*, reliability is part of the specification and it can therefore be argued that reliability is an attribute or quality. On the other hand, it depends on compliance with all the other requirements, so that quality is the fundamental basis for the achievement of reliability. Arguments on this are not important as long as the basic significance is understood.

All who propose to write specifications should consult the *Guide*, if only to be reminded of the many facets to specification, over and above mere attributes or properties. Appendix 2 gives the list of substantive clauses extracted from this publication.

Standardisation practice

Reasons for standardising. Standardisation is a procedure adopted for a number of reasons, some of which are well known and some less well known and understood. These include:

1   To stipulate a suitability for purpose.
2   To reduce the number of varieties.
3   To provide for special requirements or properties—for example, safety.
4   To increase the number of sources of supply.
5   To reduce stock holding.
6   To permit interchangeability.
7   To establish a datum for development.
8   To provide inspectability.
9   To reduce first cost.

These are not, of course, all the possible reasons; some are interdependent in particular cases and not in others; but they are enumerated for the purpose of illustrating that standardisation is not a single and narrow activity. Furthermore, whenever standardisation has been decided upon, it must be on the basis of a requirement which falls into at least one of the above categories; and those who are involved must monitor the results of the project with the object of justifying the originally declared aims.

Reviews of the results should be made formally, either continuously or at stated intervals, in order to check the degree to which the aims in the above categories are being fulfilled or, if necessary, for decisions about modifications, or even discarding the procedure. For standardisation, like many other activities, must not be performed for its own sake, or because it is the fashion, but only because it achieves something.

Objectives of standardisation. The usual objective of standardisation is economy. In terms of finance, this may not necessarily be the same as lower first cost. Longer life or higher quality of performance may give better value for money and provide an annual economy even when the first cost is higher. The test for economy is in gains over a period, in lower bills for power, in greater output per unit of power, and in reduced outlay for materials or for stockholding, etc.

In the case of reason 1 for standardisation, it may well be that, before standardisation, equipment or products (or services) then available were unsuitable for the purpose, or less suitable than could be desired. In the case of 3, however, mandatory requirements, such as legal safety stipulations, may involve higher first costs. Even then, standardisation is the best means of achieving the special requirement at the least cost, and the overall economy should be considered in terms beyond those merely financial, such as the improvement in safety.

Economy can also be effected by standardisation in terms of equivalent manpower saving, the saving of space and time, the opportunities for fewer errors, the provision of wider competition, the easier achievement of levels of quality, the facility of control for uniformity and consistency, and so on.

Special effects of standardisation in large organisations

In standardising in a large organisation, all concerned—that is, those originating the standardisation and those adopting the relevant practice —have to note that the object to be achieved, which is related to the

65

original reasons for the project, is for the benefit of the organisation *as a whole.*

In any one particular part of the organisation, it might be possible to achieve greater efficiency or economy locally by departing from the standard and using tailor-made or specialised equipment, components, materials, or methods, as the case may be. Were this behaviour to be adopted throughout the organisation, however, it would be tantamount to reverting to the situation before standardisation. That situation was deemed (by measurement) to have been less economic or beneficial than that which would result from the standardisation. It was one in which overall arrangements for purchasing, production, storage, etc, or for service, were unnecessarily complex or uneconomical. Hence, it may have to be made clear to that particular part of the organisation, that the unavoidable lowering of performance in that area is acceptable as a corollary of achieving a greater overall gain for the whole organisation.

Another manner in which standardisation may have local effects is when it involves some simplification or advantage in purchasing procedure. Besides providing economies as a result of purchasing fewer varieties in greater quantities, for example, advantage can be taken of a discount or a reduction in price as a result of purchasing a rounded-off quantity, even if higher than that actually required. It may then be necessary to persuade a part of the organisation to use this extra quantity, not because it is best technically, but because it might cost little or nothing and the overall economy could be great.

These are some features of standardisation that are particularly applicable to large organisations. Unless provision is made for adequate instruction and communications, they may not be fully appreciated at local levels of use. Indeed, lack of that appreciation is often the cause of friction between the actual users and their colleagues in purchasing departments. Hence, the increased necessity for successfully introducing standardisation into a large organisation, to make the objectives clear, to provide instruction and safeguards, and, most particularly, for some measures of enforcement.

Means of achieving standardisation

Specification as an instrument of policy. The most important and most usual instrument of standardisation policy is the specification. A specification has been described as a formal and unambiguous statement of requirements. As such it is, therefore, an ideal means of communication of needs. Referring to the various reasons for standardisation, it will be seen that it is nearly always possible to utilise a specification to express the detailed requirements of the standardisation activity, whatever it is. In fact, the best means of introducing a standard of any kind, be it an article or a method, is undoubtedly by the use of a specification. The enforcement of any standardisation policy is most easily achieved in this way.

When a specification is issued throughout an organisation, it should be against a background previously prepared by description of, and instruction in, the policy for which the specification is the instrument. For example, the policy could state that:

1 All specifications issued within the organisation must be treated as mandatory.
2 Any requests for exemption from some or all of the requirements of any specification must be made to a single (named) authority.
3 They must be accompanied by all necessary and relevant information, technical and economic, etc.
4 Exemptions would only be granted in exceptional circumstances and for a stated period.
5 They would automatically lapse at the end of the period unless a further request for exemption had been made in time—and then granted after a new consideration.

The mere tedium of having to assemble the necessary supporting information for an exemption request, and the knowledge of the difficulty of obtaining one, tends to inhibit applications and promote attempts to support the standardisation.

Formulation procedures. It stands to reason that, in issuing a specification as an instrument of policy, it should have been constructed with very great care in the first place. Trouble taken to enforce standardisation is completely wasted if it is later proved that the requirements specification has not been carefully thought out or has been based on an inadequate knowledge of practicabilities and local requirements.

A specification should therefore be made in various stages of draft. Each is given full circulation to all concerned, users and manufacturers, to ensure consultation and a complete knowledge of all the possible implications and effects. All comments received are considered carefully and action decided as a result; this may be acceptance and incorporation, or discarding. Accompanying any new draft, however, is a statement as to the reasons for taking that action. In this way, the specification receives tacit acceptance during its construction, and its ultimate issue is virtually assured of the collaboration required by the standardisation policy.

Company specifications are documents of such importance that they must be laid out and published in a suitable form, and arrangements, preferably of standardised character themselves, made for numbering, classification, and binding, etc. Amendments and modifications, when necessary, have to be issued in such a manner that all using the specification are aware that it is the most up-to-date version. Various procedures can be used to achieve this, but all are based on the requirement to keep records of the circulation. They should, preferably, be supplemented by the issue at intervals of tabular lists of specifications, amendments, and revisions.

Codes of practice. Where no specification exists, where one may take a long time to prepare, or where a specification can only refer to certain features and is not comprehensive, it may be useful to fulfil a standardisation policy by means of a code of practice. This is a document which generally refers to activities rather than to details of equipment. It can, however, be designed to point to the relevant and significant features of the latter.

Normally, a code of practice is a document of recommendations and helpful suggestions, but it can include definite instructions and mandatory requirements where these are considered to be necessary in standardisation (or in operating at all successfully) or where, for example, they may be required by law.

A code of practice must be carefully written and constructed by means of a series of consultative stages as with a specification. Since it includes both recommendatory and mandatory features, these must be clearly differentiated. The method of differentiation most favoured is by means of proper and simple phraseology, and this should have been defined in any statement of policy issued to cover the use of codes of practice or specifications (or both). For example, the policy statement indicates that all clauses using the words "shall" and "must" are mandatory throughout the organisation and are required in all cases; and that they are controlled by an exemption procedure also described and detailed in the policy. Similarly, all clauses governed by the words "should," "may," or "might" are recommendations of greater or lesser strength. It is expected that they will be obeyed wherever possible, but local circumstances or common sense will dictate any decision to act otherwise. There is no question in these cases of a formal exemption procedure.

On this matter of mandatory or recommendatory practice it is of vital importance that no prejudice is attached to the latter, so that operating in any other way is frowned upon, or favour shown to those who accept the recommendations. This would tend to make the practices which are recommendatory into mandatory ones. Unfortunately, this situation is a feature of some governmental requirements which tend to favour the acceptance of recommendations, whether justified by the circumstances or not. If a recommendation is of great value, it should be considered whether or not it would be better to raise it to the status of a mandatory requirement with the appropriate safeguards or loopholes.

The advantages of using codes of practice include the facility they provide for gaining useful experience to enable the subsequent formulation of specifications of some or all of the requirements. The specification is a more powerful instrument than a code of practice.

All instruments of standardisation policy, in whatever form, must be reviewed continuously in the light of experience fed back. They contribute in this way to the general atmosphere of control of quality and provide yardsticks for the measurement of benefits.

Procedures in the case of departures from specification by user and manufacturer

This is probably one of the most controversial aspects of quality achievement; what to do or which procedures to adopt in cases of inability to follow a standardisation policy or of non-compliance with a specification by a manufacturer for one reason or another. Lest the reader take exception even to the title of this section, it should be stated immediately, clearly and unambiguously, that, in connection with manufacture, the customer is entitled to receive goods or services or whatever is involved, strictly compliant with his stipulations in every case. If he purchases a hundred machines or a hundred biscuits he is absolutely entitled to receive a hundred good machines or biscuits. True, there are sometimes slip-ups or accidents of manufacture and a defective unit creeps in, notwithstanding inspection, but in these cases the correct procedure is replacement or rectification. No manufacturer has the right to impose on his customer an obligation to accept, say, 95 per cent compliance (because of his methods of control of quality). Unless there has been a contractual agreement to this effect, the customer pays for and expects, 100 per cent acceptability. *Caveat emptor!*

For these reasons, *never*, in any document related to the stipulation of quality, should there be included any reference to departures from that quality. This is particularly true of specifications, codes of practice, and manuals of quality control procedure. By all means, let there be mutual contractual agreements elsewhere if the circumstances demand, but the specification itself, and the manual or other document of procedure, must be rigorously fixed in relation to the ultimate achievement of quality, with no alternative acceptable. In the same way, the specified requirements of a standardisation policy on a user organisation are issued in unique terms. No alternatives are given. However, because it is not always possible to obey strictly to the letter, there may have to be means, outside the specification (or instrument of policy), by which practicable operation can proceed.

There are three main sets of circumstances in which departure from specified quality is involved. These can be put under headings as follows:

1   Exemptions.
2   Manufacturing permits.
3   Concessions.

Exemptions. Exemptions are the internal considerations of a large customer whose activities are widespread and varying, and in whose organisation a specified product or procedure has been made mandatory. This could be by instruction by internal policy, or as a direct or indirect result of an external legal or safety requirement. The purchase may have been made "globally" on behalf of all the users in the organisation. In spite of all possible pressures to ensure standard practice, there are certain areas or localities where the product or procedure in question is unsuitable technically for its purpose. It is rare for every user to be able immediately to adopt an imposed standard and to change his practice, although for economic reasons it has been necessary to insist on *adaptation* to the use of that standard. In these cases, because there exists a command requiring the use of the standard, it becomes necessary to seek a relaxation by means of an exemption from the requirements (or a particular requirement) of the specification.

Because it has been a policy decision to standardise, exemptions cannot be agreed to for other than the most urgent reasons. A mere request is useless and must be turned down. The procedure requires such a request to be detailed and accompanied by the technical reasons for making it. These enable the request to be examined rationally at technical level and recommendations made to the appropriate authority. They also provide a feed of information measuring the merits of the standardisation policy, both technically and economically. In relation to the specification itself, its value or the need for an adjustment are also demonstrated.

The authority agreeing or denying the request for exemption should preferably be the originator of the instruction or his delegated representative. This is necessary because every exemption agreed reduces the benefits of the standardisation decision. It is of the utmost importance, therefore, not to agree an exemption except for unavoidable circumstances. The circumstances will have been analysed, where necessary, by competent personnel and the pros and cons made available to the authority for a final decision. Except, possibly, for relatively trivial or unimportant standardisation decisions, the power of granting exemption should rest on one man only; this ensures uniformity and fairness. The whole procedure, however, must be strictly formal and recorded carefully.

Exemptions, where granted, should normally be for a prescribed period, before the end of which a further request for exemption, if necessary, must be made; and the document of exemption should state clearly that the request is granted for the period X to Y.

The intentions behind the choice of a fixed period should be well known. These are, first, the requirement that circumstances calling for exemption be examined carefully by the user to try to make an adaptation to come into line with the standardisation policy. Second, it provides a sufficient time to make the change economically where this was otherwise not feasible. Third, it ensures that the whole exemption system is kept under formal review and not allowed to relax indefinitely.

Exemptions are for users, and refer to departures from a policy. They must be rigorously controlled by formal means and granted only *in extremis* by top authority. The organisation for this purpose and the reasons for its adoption should be made as clear to all concerned as its relation to the standardisation policy within which it appears.

Manufacturing permits. These are sought by the manufacturer and are concerned with the period *before* actual manufacture. They are, in fact, permits requested by the manufacturer from the customer, to allow him to proceed with manufacture which will result in a departure from the specification. Reasons for requiring manufacturing permits include the saving of time or money, as when a specified material is unobtainable within a reasonable time, or when the manufacturer has a similar material in stock and can offer a price advantage, or when to process the product in a manner specified is not practicable at a particular time.

The customer has to view requests for a manufacturing permit with gravity, for his original agreement with the manufacturer was for the supply of something specific and the latter is in effect attempting to break, or at least to bend, the terms of the contract. Had the supply been proceeding for a long time, and if the permit was requested as a result of a sudden shortage of materials, a breakdown of a machine or similar *unforeseen* circumstances, then the customer ought to be sympathetic. If, however, it was a case of a new, rather than a renewed, contract, permits would normally be denied. It is no use the manufacturer claiming not to be fully aware of the requirements or details of the specification, for it was his responsibility to become so before agreement was reached. He should have clarified any possible ambiguity and have reached mutual understanding with the customer. Only in cases where the circumstances may have changed between the time of agreement and the commencement of manufacture can such a request be considered. Such a consideration would include the cost and nuisance to the customer, both of receiving something not strictly in accordance with his requirements, and also of putting into use that which may be less suitable for purpose, less safe, or less reliable, and with a shorter life. This cost and nuisance must then be compared with that involved in starting again and trying to obtain exactly compliant equipment or products elsewhere—if this is possible.

In cases where a new circumstance has become revealed to the supplier, not as a result of failure to consider the specification or other contractual obligations, but as a result of a preliminary process of design, development, or manufacture, consultation should take place. An alternative method or design may have suddenly presented itself as a possible mutual advantage. Under these circumstances, the permit should take the form of a request for a temporary or a permanent adjustment to the specification, which can only be agreed by the customer as a result of satisfactory proof that his purposes or intentions will not be reduced.

Unless a mutual agreement of this nature is reached, the price is reviewed in the light of the receipt of goods other than those ordered. Normally, the arrangements are such that the manufacturer will find it more profitable to revert to the supply of compliant goods.

Concessions. Like manufacturing permits, concessions are the concern of the manufacturer, but differ in as much as they refer to the period *after* manufacture. They may be requested by the manufacturer from the customer in cases where, by accident of manufacture, or failure of control of quality, or by faulty packing, storage, or transport, the goods ultimately received by the customer are marginally non-compliant with specification. They may also arise because the test equipment used by the manufacturer for control, has suddenly departed from calibration and, on checking by the customer, the goods prove to be defective.

It is important in the control of quality that equipment used for these purposes is kept in good order, but there are cases where there may be an unnoticed change. The customer is entitled to assume that steps are taken to maintain test equipment correctly, and should have assured himself that this is the case in selecting a supplier; but there are still occasional unforeseen lapses. As always, it is the manufacturer's responsibility to ensure the correct and uniform supply of his own raw materials, but sometimes it is not practicable to test everything and, in other instances, it is not possible—as in the case of the use of destructive testing for this purpose.

Normally, the customer requires replacement, rectification, or compensation for non-compliant goods. This is particularly so when the departures from specification are significant, but it is his right by contract even in the case of minor departures, unless otherwise agreed because of intrinsic difficulty, etc.

The first step to be taken in dealing with requests for concession, as indeed with all departures from specification, is to establish the truth for mutual agreement. This may involve independent examination, but the end result must always be agreement between supplier and customer as to what is the exact quality of the supply and to what extent it departs from the originally agreed requirements.

Notwithstanding the customer's rights to require exactly what was stipulated, he may again, as in the case of a request for a manufacturing permit, have to make a decision depending on cost and nuisance. He

73

might be able to use a slightly defective product in a certain location where conditions are less arduous than elsewhere; or he may accept a lower performance or a shorter life merely in order to preclude possibly higher losses incurred by not having the use of the goods. However, the manufacturer is in the wrong and price agreements should be reviewed, punitively where necessary, although always having regard to the facts and circumstances leading to the partial failure.

A frequent form of request for concession overlaps with one for manufacturing permit in that the need may arise after a part of the manufacture has taken place. The request may be to continue production or finish something which, it is now known, will turn out to be marginally non-compliant and on which much time and money have been spent. This, and any request for departure from specification for other reasons, must always be referred to the contracting parties since the contract is affected.

It is bad practice, although unfortunately all too commonplace, for a foreman in a production department to telephone a relatively junior member of the customer's staff in order to agree a departure, though justified or acceptable under the conditions prevailing. Subsequently, the customer is angry that the delivery is late, and the cost to the manufacturer has been increased, but neither appreciate the reasons. Therefore, all such requests should be formalised in the contractual arrangements, to the effect that any activity requested, which might affect delivery or price (as well as quality) must be suitably agreed *and recorded*, so that reference can be made to it at a later date when lateness of delivery and increased costs may be the results.

All manufacturing departures from specifications, have to be avoided by manufacturer and resisted by customer as a matter of course and contract. The references above are to rare (it is hoped) circumstances where a little elasticity may be necessary. However, it is better for both the customer and the manufacturer to rely on a specification which includes the widest possible tolerances, choice of materials and methods, consistent with suitability for purpose, and rigorously narrow only where this is necessary. This latter requirement is usually the prerogative of the customer on whom may devolve a performance or safety stricture. Finally, it is the customer's responsibility to take whatever steps are necessary to ensure that he is entrusting his orders to suppliers who are capable of providing him with full satisfaction and, in particular, compliance with his specifications—and not have to rely on procedures involved in any of the above departures.

Reasons for not standardising

Standardisation is for a purpose and, before arriving at a decision to go ahead, it is important to examine both the probable advantages and the probable disadvantages in the areas in which standardisation is to take place. A proposal to standardise may sometimes have to be refused where it can be shown that there is no advantage in proceeding.

The most usual reasons for not standardising are in the cases of products, equipment, or procedures which have to be tailor-made to suit particular and different sets of circumstances accurately or exactly. For standardisation militates against these. Whereas a specification is the best means of describing suitability for a single purpose, it is not so in the case of a number of slightly differing purposes unless it is diluted or reduced to provide for only certain common requirements, which may be few.

Loss in adjustment to a standard. Where the standardisation involves a product in a range of sizes, or a series of standards, each provides a level of quality which may be near to that required but not exactly the same. If, for example, it is decided to stock cylindrical bars of metal in sizes 1, 2, 3, 4, 6, 8, and 10 cm diameter, a requirement for exactly 4·5 cm diameter would necessitate choosing the 6 cm standard and machining it to the desired size. In the course of this action there are losses due to:

1   The costs of the superfluous and wasted material.
2   The labour, capital, and other charges involved in the machining.

The losses, in total, are called the "loss in adjustment" to the standard and must be balanced against the economic gains expected from the adoption of the standard. Ranges of standards, such as the example above, tend to have bigger gaps in the larger sizes, so the l.i.a. also tends to increase at this end of the series.

Complex structures and cumulative effects. The converse of loss in adjustment is found in the necessity for the use of standard units in a range, during the construction of a complex system. For a structure using steel girders, the latter would have been chosen *theoretically* on the basis of strength, and the weights corresponding to the design values of strength used in determining foundation requirements. The

75

practical choice of the girders may, however, have to be made from a set of standard sizes. In each case, in order not to reduce the strength below the design values, the next higher, rather than the next lower size would be taken. The cumulative effect of the resulting weight increases would completely change the concept so redesign may have to take place, allowing for greater strength, higher weights, and more robust foundations. This cumulative effect is particularly serious in the case of aircraft where a small increase in weight requires an increase in lift, therefore more powerful engines, therefore still more weight and drag, and so on, multiplying the effects tens of times.

Thus, especially in the case of products in a range of standards, it is necessary to examine the costs and delivery times of non-standard, tailor-made, articles and compare these with the economic disadvantages of using standards which have a loss in adjustment or similar handicap. This may lead to a decision not to standardise. On the other hand, in making decisions about proposals for the standardisation of a range, the number of sizes and their placing or frequency must be chosen in the light of minimising the adjustment loss over the whole range, and most especially in the sizes of common use. Similarly, where cumulative effects are a possibility, the necessity for having a large number of standard sizes, closely spaced, should be examined against the whole question of whether standardisation is worth while or not.

Six

Role of Inspection in Ensuring Quality

The most formal parts of the actual techniques of quality control generally lie within the fields of inspection. The wider implications of inspection are probably more important than the well-recognised function.

Inspection is the "policing" action without which many of the other controls of quality, including the specification stage, may be abortive. It is not sufficient to make stipulations about requirements, design, or materials, if there are no steps taken to ensure that these are in fact embodied in the product which ultimately emerges. Inspection, as with many controls, is often thought to be a self-destroying process whose necessity ceases when all the procedures of the manufacturer are truly geared to the control of the quality of the product. This is an idealised point of view, never practicable, and assumes too simple a role for the inspector. One might just as well claim that in a perfect world there would be no need for policemen. Inspectors can be those connected with the actual manufacturing processes or those representing the interests of customers. Their functions, therefore, fall into corresponding categories.

Factory inspection

Functions of the inspector. An inspector in a factory is not directly responsible for quality; failure to recognise this fact often leads to the inefficient organisation of an inspection system. His true and direct function is to ensure compliance—the matching of what emerges, with drawings, contractual requirements, specifications, properties measured by tests and performance, etc. In this capacity, he operates most successfully when guided by the availability of this information in the

77

concrete form of documents of one kind or other, of which the most powerful is the specification. While the (designed) quality of the product has been determined at the design and development stages, and eventually fixed by specifying, the inspector has to concern himself with compliance and consistency, the continuous maintenance of that quality at the level required. If his function were to be confined merely to this requirement, he would not be playing his full part in the control of quality. The mere identification of compliant and non-compliant products is a checking process which, with no difficult stretch of the imagination, could be performed by a robot suitably fed with the necessary information.

Apart from this checking, therefore, the inspector's further important functions are to provide the data which will ultimately lead to:

1   An increase in the proportion of good products in the total production.
2   An increase in the overall quality, where desirable and usable, and
3   Checking the adequacy of the specification in so far as it is concerned with all processes including preliminary ones of materials, dimensions, and tests, etc.

Notice should be taken of the phrase "ultimately lead to" since it is important to recognise that the inspector is a go-between in all these functions; he provides the data and ensures that it is placed in the right hands.

The first function is that which enables the inspector to make his contribution to productivity increase, which can be defined as the increase in the number of units of good or saleable quality/unit of production cost. (Thus, increase is not confined to mere increase in output or rate of production.) Those to whom he must communicate information, in addition to the designers who must always be kept informed, are concerned with the production methods and processes and require to know the incidence of failures or defects that may be attributable to their sphere of interest. Inspection records suitably arranged provide this.

The second function is that in which the inspector takes an important part in development; where his records show that a higher compliance proportion could be achieved by an improvement in the properties or qualities in the design. This information is fed to the designers who add it to all similar information from different sources, but chiefly from operation, in order to assess suitability for purpose. Usually, even in cases where there is the necessary organisation and communications, that operational data is not very easy to acquire and less easy to digest. It may also require extra facilities. So the steady flow of rational information in the form of inspection records is of great significance to the designer. This is especially the case when specifications, against which the records can be matched, include means of gauging the behaviour of the product in actual service. Examples of these are tests which simulate, or can be correlated to, operation.

The third function mentioned is not only concerned with proving the specification—that is, ensuring that its interpretation into production processes is exactly what was intended—but also with adjustments to the specification to make it possibly more amenable to production. These may be the tightening or widening of tolerances, or the addition of limits where these did not exist before. Sometimes, suggestions regarding actual design changes may arise during the course of inspection. These may lead on the one hand to development in the sense of improvement in what was already adequate, or on the other hand, to modifications to the specification. This type of information must always be communicated to those responsible for design and specification. The inspector takes no action himself.

In brief, it is therefore most important that quantified inspection results are communicated to those concerned. Since the inspector himself is not to be responsible for ensuing action in these fields, it is better that the form of his records should be decided by the recipients. More likely than not, one type of arrangement would be acceptable to all interested parties in design, specification, or production fields, each concerning himself with a particular part of the record.

While the inspector is concerned with compliance with specification it is his duty to acquaint himself with all the necessary techniques for achieving this. With continuous or multiple production of any kind this would involve the making of carefully planned arrangements as to which part of the whole to inspect and how to go about the inspection. Statistical methods are important here as the optimum means of using a given amount of information. It is not intended to give details of inspection techniques, statistical quality control, and sampling schemes, since these have been adequately covered elsewhere, but there is one aspect of these which can be stressed as a direct interest to management.

Reduction of manufacturing risks. When a product is rejected by an inspection process as not being compliant with a particular requirement, time and money have been wasted. It is therefore a matter for a policy decision whether to actually manufacture to somewhat different requirements, usually higher properties than those given as a minimum, or tighter tolerances than those stipulated, so as to reduce the risks of rejection and yet not increase the costs unjustifiably.

Assuming all preliminary precautions, such as control of uniformity of raw materials, have been taken, the principal causes of rejection in the actual production processes can be divided into two classifications, random effects and trends.

Random variations causing rejection. This is a subject fully treated in all works on statistical quality control. It is based on the effects of changing atmosphere, tools not being homogeneous in sharpness, operator vagaries and a host of relatively small and usually unidentifiable differences in time. These result in products in continuous production and ostensibly the same, varying one from another within a small range of, say, dimensions.

The object of the SQC is to quantify this situation to enable corrective action to be taken. This might involve the customer modifying his specified requirements without altering his aims, or more usually the manufacturer adjusting the processes to create the probability of virtually all products emerging as acceptable.

The simplest example is that relating to tolerances on dimensions. If the specification calls for a diameter of 2 ± 0.005 cm and a properly chosen sample of products varies between 1.992 and 2.007 cm, then either the specification is re-examined to find whether 2 ± 0.010 cm would still be satisfactory (the cheapest procedure); or the process has to be refined to give, say, 1.996 to 2.003 cm, with only a remote risk of exceeding these figures on either side.

Variation as a trend towards rejection. While random variations can be handled in a logical manner by the application of statistics to the setting of the processes, trends are more difficult to control. They may arise as a result of changes taking place systematically, such as wear and tear, accelerating failure, or even by accident. The difference between properties *just* within, and those *just* outside, specification requirements is the difference between saleability and unsaleability. Therefore inspection has to be arranged by the manufacturer so as to minimise the effects of this possibly catastrophic situation.

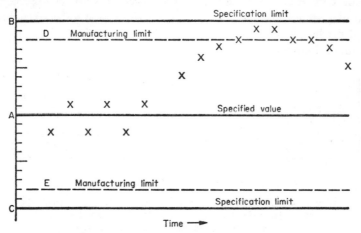

FIGURE 7   SIMPLIFIED QUALITY CONTROL CHART
Manufacturing limits set within specification limits provide a safeguard against non-compliance.

The best way, as usual, is one that can be appreciated quickly by eye. Consider the control chart shown in Figure 7 which represents the simplest and most useful type of pictorial aid in inspection. The abscissa can be time in any form, minutes, hours, or days, or serial numbers of production, 50, 100, or 150, etc. The ordinate is a scale of measurement of the relevant property, sufficiently extensive to cover all possible variations. The horizontal A is the specified value, and B and C are the specification limits, such that any value between B and C is acceptable. In order to provide a safeguard to production and reduce risk of rejection, it is decided, however, to manufacture to tighter limits D and E. The values measured, and indicated by crosses, show that production commenced satisfactorily around the actual specification value, but that the property measured began to rise with an unmistakable trend. This, if allowed to continue, might have resulted in ultimate rejection. On approaching the manufacturing limit D, however, action was called for, a warning sounded, and after a short time the trend was corrected. In the time during which correction was taking place, the *manufacturing* limit was exceeded because of the lag of events, but since this was within the *specification* limit, at no time was saleability in question.

81

Since it is restrictive to operate to tighter limits, the magnitude of manufacturing limits should be considered carefully in terms of costs against benefits. Their use, however, together with an appropriate warning system arranged to enable corrective action to be taken while still producing satisfactorily, is a good example of calculated risk to reduce rejections.

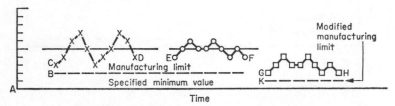

Time

FIGURE 8   CONTROL CHART FOR MINIMUM VALUE

If production variations can be reduced by better control, the manufacturing limit can be brought closer to the specified value, resulting in greater economy.

The cost of working beyond the specification can of course be reduced as a result of examination of this type of chart. Figure 8 shows a chart arranged for the case of a specified minimum value A. The manufacturing limit is B and $C - D$ shows the results of measuring a production run. Two things are noticeable about this series of values; the first is that the lowest value is satisfactorily above the manufacturing limit; the second is that the variation from maximum to minimum is about twice the magnitude of the difference between A and B. This seems a reasonable state of affairs, since, if production is geared to a mean between C and D, a half-variation will only bring it to B, and should therefore permit a safeguard in the event of any abnormal trend.

If, as a result of examining $C - D$ it is decided that production can be tightened by means of a process change, or raw materials control, the values could eventually appear as $E - F$. Here, the production aim is the same, but the variations have been considerably smoothed out. This would justify a lower production aim and a lower manufacturing limit, giving the situation as at $G - H$ and limit K, which may well be an economy in production.

The design of appropriate control charts and decisions as to limiting values are properly handled by quality control techniques. The above is a general description of procedures.

82

Organisation for factory inspection. In a factory, the most important organisational step in setting up an inspection system is to ensure that the requirements of output and those of quality are not in conflict. It is wrong, therefore, to make the chief inspector (however called) report directly and unilaterally to an executive concerned only with production interests. One cannot expect the managing director to have his burdens increased by direct responsibility for inspection, but, as an ultimate resort, the chief inspector should have access to highest management in those cases where the resolution of a conflict of interests has proved impossible at lower levels. On the other hand, the production manager, for his part, has to understand the implications of lack of quality; that quality is *his* business as well as that of the inspectors who cannot be on his staff if they are measuring his degree of success. The success or otherwise of his work will not, in the long term, be merely a matter of how much output he can achieve, but to what extent he can satisfy customers and increase profit.

In a system which ensures compliance with requirements and that filters off defective products, the factory inspector is serving the interests of both the customers and his employers. This ultimately works to the advantage and state of health of his organisation. The system should control the intake of raw materials, as well as the direct requirements of characteristics and tests concerned with the product. (Raw materials can be defined as anything brought in on which no work has yet been done by the receiver. It can include chemicals and other materials, castings, forgings, components, or even sub-assemblies.) There should be provision for the supplier of raw materials to demonstrate that he has met the stipulations required of him and, where necessary, to issue certification to that effect. Occasional checks by the receiving organisation or its agent will ensure satisfaction.

Besides the relatively technical side of inspection, the measurement and testing, the organisation should provide facilities for the efforts which can be made by commonsense (that rare attribute!) and by the use of the five senses. These should not be underestimated. Nor should provision be omitted for even the most elementary precautions of good housekeeping, such as to ensuring cleanliness, and that assembly processes are performed in good conditions and light—all helping to provide the best chance for the final stipulations to be met.

Inspection should have some influence on aspects of handling, packing, storing, and transport, and the inspection organisation be such that efforts made in production are not nullified subsequently and before the goods reach the customer. This can be achieved either by the judicious location of final inspection or by allocating the necessary powers or authority to the inspection organisation.

An inspection organisation must maintain full records not only to provide instant information for the control of quality, and for the supply of data to designers, as discussed above, but also as a reference system when a case history is required. This is of particular importance in the case of a defective product apparently slipping through the inspection system.

Finally, a note about personnel. Management must ensure that the work of factory inspectors is not too much dependent on judgement and must provide the appropriate carefully designed standards and specifications. The common practice of taking older men from possibly more strenuous jobs into inspection is not necessarily an advantage. On the one hand, they may certainly have experience and skill; but on the other hand, their sight and powers of concentration may not be as good as those of younger men. Additionally, they would have to overcome the effects of new relationships with both job and former colleagues.

Inspection by the user

A customer or user may wish to make his own inspection. The principles to be followed are the same whether he is an individual or a member of a large organisation—only the people doing the actual inspection task vary.

A large organisation is always a user. Even when it is a manufacturing organisation it has to bring in raw materials. Sometimes, however, it is purely a user in the case of some products or equipment, as in the instance of a power generating organisation buying fuel. As such, it may have an inspection body which ensures that what is purchased is according to requirements. The inspection can take place at different levels and by one or more inspectors according to the size of the organisation. Some of those levels, which in small organisation may be combined, are given later.

Inspection by the customer or user should not be necessary in the ideal case, but even when the manufacturer has fully accepted his responsibilities for quality compliance, there are always instances where the further safeguard of a check by the customer is useful. Again, although less necessary in some cases than in others, inspection by the user is one way of ensuring that his approval of the manufacturer

84

was justified and his confidence in the consistency of quality of the supply well placed.

In some instances, there may be a mandatory responsibility on the customer—for example, for safety—which is not in any way transferable. Usually this applies to a particular property rather than to the quality as a whole. In that case, the user may have to perform his own inspection for that property, irrespective of what has been done before.

Briefly, inspection by the user can consist of relatively simple examinations on receipt, normally performed in a non-technical manner by, say, a storekeeper; random full inspections of a technical nature on samples drawn from anywhere—that is, on receipt, from stores, or from usage—and the witnessing of what is going on in the field of control of quality at the point of actual manufacture.

Storekeeper's duties. Inspection proper is a technical function and an inspector normally has a comprehensive technical background to achieve best results. There are, however, simple safeguards in the "policing" sense which can be applied by the user through non-technical or semi-technical personnel. For example, a storekeeper's duty is to ensure compliance with contractual requirements in such terms as quantitative matters, delivery dates, and other conditions more or less external to the products. He should, therefore, have the necessary facilities to measure weight, volume, size (in the coarse sense), and numbers, Where visual inspection is appropriate, this must be done to observe whether the goods appear to be in an acceptable condition, free from contamination or corrosion, and not externally damaged. In appropriate cases he can actually gauge a size rather than measuring that it is a 3 cm rather than a 2 cm bar, or a number 10 rather than a number 9 boot. This gauging can even extend to fine measurement using non-measuring equipment, such as "go" and "no-go" gauges, which would enable him to act for the actual user in determining compliance and acceptability. On the other hand, tests in the usual sense of the term, should not be performed by a storekeeper.

All these checks must be done on receipt, or as soon thereafter as possible, both for commercial reasons and also to eliminate possible later effects due to inadequate storage or subsequent handling. Obviously, all these later activities must be well provided for and controlled, otherwise the care exercised in the control of quality will have been wasted.

85

Checking after receipt. Some customers prefer to make random but comprehensive checks after receipt, in order to ensure that the supplies are fully compliant with all requirements. Checking frequency should be according to the nature of the articles concerned, and also to the degree of confidence in the supplier's control arrangements. The knowledge that checks are being made, however rarely, is salutory to the supplier. They usually involve the whole of the specification and require the same technical facilities as used by the manufacturer. Thus, the responsibility for checks should be directly on the user or his (technical) representative, who have powers to draw random test samples from stores or even from usage where necessary. These tests serve to buttress the user's main inspection system (below) and also to provide a source of data on the adequacy of the products or the specification. In some cases, usually where safety is involved, the user may have responsibilities related to the use of the product. It is then required of him to make checks or to ensure that they are made for him, in regard to a particular part of a specification or other stipulation. These also verify the depth of control exercised in manufacture.

Inspection at manufacture. Far and away the most profitable inspection, especially for a large user organisation, is that performed by its inspectors or representatives visiting the actual place of manufacture. In this way, the most appropriate steps can be taken to ensure compliance at the point of productton where the actual processes are taking place. In some cases, the purchaser may require supplies to be sent to different locations, where inspection *after* receipt would require a multiplication of staff, equipment, or facilities. This would have consequential risks of possible confusion occasioned by different standards of inspection or by subjective opinions. At the same time, a number of systems of communication to handle complaints and other queries would have to be maintained. Inspection *at* manufacture virtually eliminates these complications.

Working methods of visiting inspector. Inspection visits to suppliers may be made either regularly, and at intervals determined by circumstances, or irregularly. The advantages of making irregular visits to ensure by random checks that all is well, should be weighed against the possible nuisance to the supplier or his own inspection staff. They would, after all, have to become engaged in certain formalities. In any case, even in regular visits, checks can be made on random samples if necessary.

The procedure observed should commence with (*a*) an examination of records of recent production (another advantage of inspection at manufacture)—this makes sure that the relevant controls are operating satisfactorily; next (*b*) would be the witnessing of control of quality by routine testing and checking during factory inspection, usually on a sample drawn at random from production (by himself); (*c*) the rejection for any non-compliance; (*d*) the arrangements made for identifying defectives and isolating them for removal, scrap, or re-work; and (*e*) the arrangements for the release of compliant goods.

From time to time, the visiting inspector may wish to withdraw a sample for checking outside the factory or by the user's own facilities. This helps to ensure that the factory test equipment is maintained in a proper condition and calibrated where necessary.

Normally, a user's inspector works to contract documents which include such items as specifications and drawings. These provide him with exact criteria by which he can take the necessary steps to ensure compliance or to reject. Clearly, all such documents have to be up to date, and it is bound to cause trouble if an addition or modification is agreed between supplier and customer without keeping the inspector informed.

Visiting inspection powers are to reject only; acceptance is the prerogative of the user or his purchaser who has to consider matters other than compliance, such as delivery and price. Thus, inspection is a process which permits or forbids acceptance but does not actually accept. This function can be extended, however, in the run of a contract, where commercial and other similar matters have been fixed. Acceptance can then be delegated to the inspector.

Even without formal documents a skilled visiting inspector can make large contributions to the production of satisfactory goods, and his advice, as the user's representative, is usually welcomed by the manufacturer. For this reason, it is not enough for an inspector to know the mere inspection formalities. It is an advantage for him to know the production process and the equipment for both production and control. Usually, therefore, a mechanical engineering background will be found to be the best basis for an inspector of most products, since they are all made and tested on machines.

Resident inspection. Where a supplier is producing orders of very large value for substantial periods, it was considered in the past to be of economic advantage for the user to install a permanent or semipermanent inspector at the manufacturer's works. In the case of complex machines, it was deemed that the "saving" of one would more than justify the expense involved, and that the mere presence of a supervisory eye would ensure the effectiveness of relatively simple controls of cleanliness and proper assembly, avoiding a great deal of rectification time later. It was also assumed that the resident inspector would keep the factory inspection system "on its toes."

The modern view, however, is that this type of inspection is quite unnecessary provided that there has been a thorough "vetting" process. Delegated inspection with the right appreciation of responsibility works to the advantage of both supplier and customer, and has the undoubted advantages of placing the undivided onus for quality on the supplier—that is, where it ought to be.

Delegated inspection. The inspection function of the user can be delegated to the manufacturer when it has been shown that his controls are completely satisfactory—by the resulting supply of quality. This delegation does not, of course, remove the over-riding authority of the user's inspector, nor the right of the customer to receive actually what he is paying for (not what purports to be the same). By the use of delegation, routine visits can be reduced considerably in frequency in exchange for the formal acceptance by the manufacturer of complete responsibility for quality, and the knowledge that all necessary steps to achieve this are in constant use. Associated with any system of delegated inspection are also attendant higher risks in respect of failures, and the supplier involved should always ensure that these risks are well known to those who have the appropriate responsibilities.

"Vetting" of a manufacturer. The vetting of a manufacturer in order to establish whether he is a suitable supplier or not, involves the user's inspector in a series of formalities and procedures, a record of which must be kept as a part of the "history" of any mutual relations. A standard form is usually a feature of the inspection system. It commences with the mundane details of identification, name, address, phone number (of the factory, not the head office), and names of personnel concerned. It goes on to a description of layout and general remarks about facilities and appearance. Next come remarks about the capabilities and state of production equipment, facilities for the internal control of quality, the qualifications of the control staff and their

organisational responsibilities, and the qualifications of any special personnel—for example, certificated welders. Finally, statements are made as to the forward-looking attitude of the company, its development programmes, and equipment relevant to the inquiry. This report or record ends with the inspector's own views on:

1   Rate of production possible.
2   Any shortcomings in the above.
3   Where the manufacturer may need any special help or advice in regard to particular requirements.
4   Where or how he could improve his control or other facilities *vis-à-vis* the user's proposed contractual stipulations.

Finally, a technical recommendation is made. Copies are passed to the user and the purchaser, where these are different, and to this information the latter adds the necessary commercial details, such as financial standing, before arriving at a decision with the agreement of the user, to declare the supplier suitable or not.

With this approval of a supplier, there are formalities that are designed in each case to lock the system of production and control as far as necessary into the condition in which it was examined and approved. These include, for example, the issue by the user's inspector of numbered rubber stamps to the appropriate factory inspectors. These remain the property of the user and are returnable on request or at any change of system or personnel. Any stamp on a document or release means to both parties that all the relevant requirements have been accurately observed.

It is of particular importance in vetting to ensure that the control arrangements are specifically for the particular products in consideration. It would defeat the whole object if it were possible to switch the control facilities and staff from one product for the first customer, to another for the second, when the latter's representative called. This situation can be prevented by the insistence on the maintenance of adequate records indicating that the product in question has, in fact, been in continuous control.

Factors affecting standards of inspection. Various inspection committees throughout industry and government departments have, at one time or another, considered what can be done to eliminate differences between standards of inspection. There is no obvious and certain way of achieving complete uniformity, which is especially necessary when the production is very close to specification limits, as also in the consideration of marginal non-compliances. In an ideal world, with perfect specifications, these matters would not have to be discussed, but the effects are actually more widespread than is generally realised. An article deemed to comply at the factory can sometimes be rejected by the user, even when no change has occurred in transit. For we are dealing with human beings and, sometimes, opinions.

To reduce these differences to a minimum it is necessary to consider the factors involved. These are:

1   Factors common to all manufacturers, including drawings, specifications, gauge schedules, test equipment, and contractual requirements—*in which there should be no differences.*

2   Variable factors, usually matters of interpretation but including variations in test equipment, calibration, and ambient conditions.

As with every other form of activity, however, the human element plays a significant part in determining the quality of inspection. Fatigue, interruption, or lack of concentration have to be recognised and avoided by proper controlling of inspection activities. By fatigue, of course, is meant any deterioration in the ability of the senses. Thus, a strenuous optical examination or measurement can cause errors after some repetitions, and the method should be examined with a view to simplification (reduction of strain) or to scheduling at appropriate intervals to include restoration periods.

Other ways in which the variations in inspection standards can be minimised include:

1   The careful centralisation of control of the whole system—for example, under a chief inspector.

2   The issue of inspection regulations defining the principles of inspection and occasional supplements providing detailed instructions for specific instances.

3   Checking factory inspector's instructions at the point of production.

4   Critical examination of first-off samples and, later, of any variations in routine production, as a guide to inspection procedure.

5   Periodical calibration of inspection and test equipment.

6   Elimination where possible of the human element in inspection.

Procedure for the handling of complaints. The test of a user's inspection system is not only when matters are running smoothly, and in the feed of information to all concerned, purchaser, designer, specifier, user, *and* supplier. It is most critically tested in the handling of complaints. Obviously, many complaints arise as a result of matters beyond the inspector's responsibility. These include deficiences in quantity (where this is, say, a storekeeper's field); failure in delivery; inadequate storage at the receiving end (that at the supply end should be subject to his inspection); handling; installation; and usage. It may still be useful, however, for him to receive information about some of these where the circumstances enable him to compile data which relate to his work. For example, inadequate storage or bad handling at the receiving end may result in suggestions for a change in packaging at the supply end. All such failures may have been appraised as to whether they are the responsibilities of the supplier or the customer.

In the case of complaints relating to conformance with quality requirements, which are the inspector's especial responsibility, all information from any source —for example, operation— must be passed to the inspector. It is sometimes the case, where speedy replacement or other similar action is required, that the purchaser communicates directly with the supplier. If so, the same information must go to the inspector and, as it should to the supplier, this should include as many relevant facts as possible. These might be details or measurements indicating a shortcoming from the relevant specification (or other) requirements, that are also quoted. The supplier should also receive the faulty product or a sample, or be permitted to examine it wherever it is, if he so wishes.

The most frequent result of such a complaint, especially where supported by the factual evidence, is for the supplier to agree the rectification action, replacement, re-imbursement, or other similar redress. Sometimes, however, the complaint may be very marginal or possibly ill-founded. For neither party has the prerogative of being wrong. The supplier may then wish to challenge by performing his own tests, and produce a case history justifying his challenge. The inspector should then take over the situation, using all means to establish the truth and ensure that there is mutual acceptance of this. All facilities must be provided for the supplier to enable him to make further tests where necessary, and much commonsense has to be exercised when decisions have to be made about the costs of tests and the transport of supposedly faulty goods. Once the truth has been agreed, commercial matters can be taken up and the inspector can add to his records of performance of the supplier, as necessary.

Inspector's programmes of visits. An inspector operating on behalf of a user must travel to factories. It is necessary to minimise the time and expense occupied in doing so, in order to increase his productive efficiency. This can be defined, roughly, as the time of performing actual inspection duties, divided by the total "working" time. All steps must be taken to achieve this and in particular the following points are worthy of examination:

1   To minimise total travelling time, he should live at or near to the "centre of gravity" of his region. This can be found by marking the factories to be visited on a map and choosing the point which gives least total mileage. It can be refined by "weighting" the factories in terms of importance, or annual value of orders, or the necessity for different frequencies of visits.

2   To reduce travelling cost to a minimum also, the means of travel have to be considered. Usually, a car is necessary to the saving of both time and money—but this is not always the case and depends on the geography and size of the region.

3   Wherever possible his schedule of visits should be planned and arranged in advance and his location at any time reasonably known. This may be, in the case of a large user, for the benefit of the chief inspector or his representative at headquarters.

4   Since the value of inspection depends on the keeping of records and the circulation of reports, it is necessary for an inspector to spend a certain fixed time in his office, wherever that is, in order to maintain his paper work in an organised state. This could be certain hours in the day, or a certain day in the week. It should be fixed in such a manner as to permit contact—for example, from headquarters—or simplify the allocation of part of the time of a clerical or typing assistant.

5   It may be that the inspector visits a less important supplier before another because it is near at hand. There may be a limited time left in a working day which, unless used in this way—that is, to visit a factory conveniently near to that already visited—would otherwise be wasted.

6   The requirement of a change to a scheduled programme should only be made in emergency. It has to be remembered that

scheduled visits are expected, have to be prepared for at factories, and may involve a certain discontinuity in routine production tasks.

Personal qualities of a visiting inspector. An inspector is a man (or woman) of high responsibility; character and personality are, therefore, matters of great importance. He must be a man of integrity and authority, with the realisation, in the case of the user's inspector, that when on premises not his own, he will see and learn things, however trivial and apparently unimportant, which must be maintained as confidential. A visiting inspector who utilises facts from one supplier to help his competitor is failing in his duty. On the other hand, there is no harm in him putting the two suppliers into communication in the event that *they* have no objection to exchanging information.

He must ensure that any instructions which he gives on behalf of the customer, and which fall within his responsibilities and the contractual arrangements, are carried out to the letter, and that if they are not, the most senior authorities on both sides are made aware of the facts.

While aiming to work amicably with all suppliers, too much "fraternisation" should, if possible, be avoided for obvious reasons. Those responsible for devising inspection schedules should give serious consideration to periodical interchanges of inspectors which, however, must not affect the inspection efficiency.

On occasion, an inspector must understand the possible reluctance of a supplier to allow him to see all processes. For there may be a secret which the supplier, rightly, wishes to preserve. In this case, it is only necessary for the inspector to concern himself with the quality and consistency of the final product, all activities and records for the demonstration of which must be contractually acceptable. On the other hand, the supplier must understand the possible risk he is taking, in denying an inspector full facilities, that he may lose orders to a competitor more forthcoming.

Seven

Development I: Improvement and Innovation

Development cannot be achieved without measurement, and if performance or a function has to be achieved, measurement involves testing. Technical advances invariably follow testing and measurement, in their widest connotations and by whomever performed, provided the right use is made of the results.

Development for improvement

Development is generally embarked upon for some improvement. This might be in performance, life, or cost, or any or all of a large number of features which may be desirable. To measure improvement, however, requires a knowledge of two things: (*a*) the value of the starting point, norm, or datum, and (*b*) the subsequent change in value.

To be able to say that machine *A* is cheaper than machine *B* obviously requires a knowledge of the cost of each. Similarly, to say that machine *A* is "better" than machine *B* also requires knowledge of the quantified features by which the comparison is made. It would not be possible to claim a longer life for one unless the lives of both had been measured and compared. For these reasons, one of the important functions of standardisation is to provide a datum from which to measure a constant quality which is used as a starting point for development. This is dealt with elsewhere. The approach to development must therefore be made fully mindful of the necessity for thorough quantifications rather than subjective impressions.

Actual methods of testing are not described, but the different general

94

types are discussed and attempts made at indicating the relative merits of, the precautions to be observed in, and what can be expected from, each type. However, whatever the tests, if used for development they will have been wasted unless the subject of the tests is improved in one way or another as a result. The improvement can take many forms, such as in actual performance or in greater consistency at the same level of performance. Whenever, after a programme of development testing, the results indicate a reduction in performance, an earlier failure, a lower adequacy for purpose, time and money will have been wasted, intentionally or not.

It is therefore useful, whenever possible, to institute a preliminary period of simple and speedy checks, tests, or trials to provide a first assessment of the likelihood of success with subsequent and more comprehensive testing. This is particularly necessary before embarking on extensive operational trials, when such precautions as tests for materials, properties, any similar stipulations by specification or otherwise, correct assembly, proper kinematic relationships, static and/or dynamic load tests, and so on, must be made. Any other steps which can be conveniently taken must also be included in preliminary checks which, in the aggregate, are designed to prevent waste of time and money overall.

In these ways, it is ensured as far as possible that equipment or products (or modifications thereto) which are to be subjected to examinations of long-term performance, reliability or life tests, are likely to be more advantageous than those in previous use. This is true development—trial and success, not trial and error. Any organisation or company which makes a claim to be performing development must base it on this procedure. The claim can only be justified by the demonstration of facilities and means of eliminating from consideration, any equipment which is liable not to be an improvement on that hitherto used. The awarding of a development contract to a company should always be contingent on this, and not on the ability to make designs, drawings or prototypes conveniently or at a faster rate.

Development for innovation

There is a second aspect to development that is different from the above one of continuing improvement. This goes beyond the examination of existing equipment and practices to the examination of requirements, and is more concerned with new departures and particularly the overturning of "sacred cows" and fixed routines. From time to time, and for various reasons, not least profitability, it may be necessary to commence with a fresh mind and revert to the fundamental requirements. The attitude to adopt in these cases, is to recognise that it is not the equipment or means which are important so much as the ends or job to be done—the true purpose. No amount of improvement in the quality or reliability of the cross-bow would have produced a machine gun; no amount of study for the design of better buttonholes would have resulted in the zip fastener. Thus, at all stages of development, the job to be done must be kept in the forefront of the considerations. The process is related to value analysis, which is concerned with achieving the exact purpose most economically. There are many interesting techniques and procedures which can be adopted, and also much expense to be saved, by design teams looking at a product and asking "what has it to do exactly?" When there is no product as yet, the same question is the starting point of the programme.

Even in this type of development, however, it is extremely rare to be able to arrive at the satisfactory solution in only one step. This would have been ideal design work rather than development, which implies a dynamic situation, a growth. Instead of a programme in which improvement is sought to an existing product already providing some measure of satisfaction to customers, the situation is one in which improvement is sought to prototypes (or first drafts, attempts, or embodiments of intentions) in order to arrive ultimately at satisfaction. This requires testing no less than the first and more usual kind of development, both during the programme itself and also at the end point. The latter is especially necessary to ensure that the objectives have actually been achieved.

Thus, the dominating feature of all development is testing in controlled circumstances.

Development policy as it affects, and is affected by, middle management

Before actually dealing with the various types of testing used in development, it is worth noting that those who are involved should not only be personnel specifically qualified and chosen for the job, but also other key figures in an organisation.

Obviously the actual programmes, techniques, and tasks will be performed by the specialists, but it is unwise in the extreme to segregate these in such a way that other people, say routine production management, refer to them as the "long-haired" or "back-room" boys.

Everyone should know the general lines of thought towards development; everyone must be able to appreciate any changes which may be going on. Middle management, in particular, should be involved in development not merely in hiring, firing, or transferring men. It is too rarely realised that the main sources of development requirements are those who make, use, and require things—not the development experts.

As an example of how this works, assume that as a first approximation, the success of a manufacturing firm is measured by profit. Monitoring of mere turnover or sales volume is then made into an activity allied with, or related in some way to, profit. It is then management's duties to look for profitable activities and profitable products, to increase their own performance. If, for example, the products are sold by quantity—that is, by weight, volume, area, and length—the material content of the overall cost may be large. It is often the case that this type of product hardly involves any great measure of skill or knowledge; even when it does, its nature is such that competition quickly catches up, with the ultimate result of a reduction in any benefit, and a loss of advantage.

Steel, sold by weight in the form of plate, sheet, rods, bars, or girders, brings a price per ton which reflects the dominance of the material element. If it is made into razor blades, the price per ton is increased by about 500 times, if made into an aero engine, 5000 times. While nothing is implied here as to the actual profitability of these three examples, there is no doubt that there is a greater opportunity for profit when one departs from the sale by weight of an elementary product. So the most important commodity in a product is technology. All efforts should be bent towards this achievement—how to produce and sell products with high "know-how" content; how to discard or gradually replace those which do not fall into this category. If the latter are admittedly "paying the rent" or making a contribution towards subsistence, this will only be the case until such a time as somebody else makes them quicker, cheaper, or better.

As a general spur to development, therefore, middle management must be involved in these concepts and the lines of policy corresponding. They will then understand and appreciate the necessity for changes which may be called for, in addition to the obvious importance of eliminating waste of time, materials, and labour. They will usually support changes themselves. Short cuts which may have to be taken into a new field of production, such as arrangements for temporary supplies from another source, will be obvious as the natural consequences of the priority given to profit over mere production.

Development by means of standardisation

Standardisation involves a very wide field of activities ranging from a simple rationalisation to the writing of a comprehensive specification. It is often adopted as a matter of policy for one particular set of reasons —for example, simplification of stock holding—and rejected for another —for example, "too much standardisation stultifies development." The latter, quite widely held view, has often been used to oppose the provision of resources of men, money, and equipment for standardisation activities. Those engaged in these fields often come up against this argument.

It is an argument which appears to be neither irrational nor surprising, since clearly the two words "standardisation" and "development" seem to have contradictory implications. The dictionary gives the first as a *fixing* to an established criterion, and the second as a gradual *growth*. Thus, standardisation is related to a static, whereas development is related to a dynamic, situation and the two fields, therefore, appear at first sight to be incompatible. Nevertheless, it can be shown that this need not be the case if the proper approaches are made. Those long experienced in development work, are aware that the use of standardisation to increase the rate of development has become a most powerful technique. The solution to this apparent paradox lies in the adoption of methods of application of standardisation procedures in a dynamic and not a static manner.

It has been shown that standardisation is embarked upon for a particular reason or number of reasons. This may simply be the establishment of a suitability for purpose by means of the drawing up of a specification, or the reduction in too great a number of varieties of articles in stock by simple rationalisation. However, if it is to be effective, there must be some subsequent checking to provide quantitative justification for the original intentions or plan. Standardisation activities cannot be taken on trust; there have to be reviews to ensure that the quality *is* right for the purpose, that the numbers of varieties *have* been reduced, and that stock holdings *have* become smaller and more economical. It is this continual reviewing following the introduction of some standardisation practice which provides the facilities for creating a dynamic situation which is therefore compatible with the furthering of development. Needless to say, it requires the setting up of suitable means of communication between those responsible for the results in actual practice and those responsible for the original preparation and the subsequent review of the standardisation itself.

To illustrate how a dynamic situation is set up it is easiest to consider the standardisation as creating a criterion of quality—although the argument is equally applicable to any of the other practices that are labelled "standardisation."

In general, by the very nature of things, all commodities and products tend to improve as time elapses. If one could draw a graph of quality, however expressed, against time, the line would have a generally upward trend as shown in Figure 9.

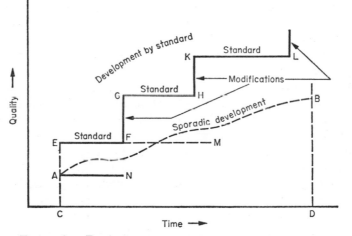

FIGURE 9   DEVELOPMENT BY MEANS OF STANDARDISATION

Standards periodically upgraded provide a platform for more rapid quality improvement than a continuous but casual process of development.

The quality at time C is represented by the ordinate AC and that at a later time D by BD, the sporadic development being the dotted line AB. This is usually uneven according to the immediate reasons for quality change; the pressures of purchasers, competition from rivals, or natural growth factors such as may be grouped under the general heading of experience. Although there is an upward trend, there are occasional reductions in quality which may be due to lack of control or badly organised attempts at development. The principal feature of this uncontrolled increase in quality, however, is its irregularity.

If, instead of allowing this state of affairs to continue, it is decided at time C to standardise by establishing a quality criterion, that criterion is higher than any such as AC, hitherto available. The reason for this is simply that, in setting up a procedure for standardisation, it is necessary to examine the features of existing products. Where there are a number of product variants available, clearly attempts are made to exclude from the standard any technical shortcomings of particular ones, and, wherever possible, to include in the standard the best features of existing variants. Compensation would be a feature of the final specification which would be represented in quality as the ordinate EC. The arguments about stultying development are shown to be false immediately, owing to this simple fact. The proper approach and investigation ensures that the first attempt at a standard is representative of a better quality (or value for money) than anything otherwise available at the time.

The initial standard is now used for some length of time as a fixed or static criterion. This certainly rationalises commercial procedures, especially purchasing, but the most important feature of the period, shown as EF in the diagram, is that technical procedures are rationalised. If it is used to keep the standard under review, to feed information from users to standardisers, that operational data is known to relate to a fixed datum of quality and not to a range of qualities. The mere existence of a specification enables the facilities for inspection to provide an assurance that, indeed, the product is controlled to a uniformity, which might not have been the case otherwise. The specification has become a platform for development.

At time F, a considerable amount of information has been accumulated, all relatable directly to a fixed criterion, and showing that improvements can or ought to be made. Modifications are therefore made to the specification, raising the quality to G. Commercial and other arrangements are reviewed in the light of this change, and purchasing again proceeds stably on the basis of quality G for a further period, GH, during which operating data is again fed back to maintain the review of the standard. It may not be advisable to introduce modifications too frequently, although it is possible that the original criterion was less than perfect at the time and soon requires an urgent change. In that case, the modification can be issued in the form of an addendum to the current specification, and at a time convenient to all parties concerned. When a number of modifications of this nature have accumulated or require to be introduced, it is necessary, subject to cost and expediency, to re-issue the specification in a new edition incorporating them.

It may well be asked how it can be ensured that a revision upwards takes place at F rather than at M, a time at which the development would have lagged behind the natural or free development. (In passing, it should be noted that even then the purchasing and other commercial advantages of operating with a standard commodity might override the possible gains from minor development.) This rarely happens, however, since proper consideration of even the basic data available at time C in the light of the organised collection of information from that time onwards, creates a pressure for change greater than that from casual operation. The important requirement is communication; the users must know the thinking behind the standardisation in order that they can present their operational data in a development form.

The whole process is in the nature of a series of steps. Static periods of operation occur in the times EF, GH, KL, with provision of the dynamic element by the introduction of improvements $F-G$, $H-K$, etc. The organised method of procedure, the possibility of relating information exactly to an unchanging criterion for a certain length of time, and the feeding of operational data into the products by way of a change in specification, always produce a rate of ascent or development which is greater overall than that due to the sporadic development.

One word of caution must be mentioned here. The process described is a development procedure intended for those involved in development, normally technical personnel. Where this is not the case—where, for instance, the decision to standardise is purely a purchasing matter—great care has to be taken to adopt a similar procedure of examining all variants and arriving at a compromise of the best elements. Suppose, for immediate commercial advantage or simple convenience, it were decided to standardise on an existing product of quality AC. Fixing the position without feed-back of data would create the line $A-N$, certainly lagging behind possible sporadic development. With no technical procedures, the quality would become relatively lower as time advances. At the time N, improvement may be forced by the pressure of external casual development, but this would only bring the quality to that level, not higher. Hence, development by the use of standardisation is conditional on the necessity for:

1   Standards being made, by whomever, on generally technical considerations.

2   Great care being taken when a standard is made as a result of first cost considerations only.

3   Standardisation being operated as a dynamic, rather than a static process—that is, standards kept under constant review to check against the original intentions.

If these attitudes are adopted, the apparent incompatibility vanishes and standardisation provides an extremely powerful instrument for development.

Types of testing

Operational testing. No tests are as satisfactory and convincing as those which comprise actual operations by the user, for his purposes, in the intended (and sometimes, accidental) environment—with the addition of a monitoring (measuring and recording) procedure. This can vary from mere observation and the keeping of a log or record, to full instrumentation. Observation has to be performed by a suitably trained and skilled observer; and, where possible, the instrumentation should be of a type which either automatically records continuously, or enables this type of record to be kept. Whatever the cost of operational testing procedure, cost is added to the operations, and as always, and especially in the case of expenditure on so-called (wrongly) non-productive activities, this has to be justified in the light of the value gained, and the best compromise reached.

To get the most value for the least expenditure, it is necessary, first of all, to make decisions as to what is significant information and what may be of mere passing interest. This is sometimes an extremely difficult task. It should therefore be reviewed from time to time, having regard to the experience of subsequent analyses. What may have appeared insignificant at first, or what may have received no consideration at all, can prove to be of the utmost value in relation to the behaviour of the equipment in use. Looking at the cost, the value of the increasing accumulation of information may not only accrue to the user directly, but, in more cases than not, also to the supplier or manufacturer. Rational information about actual operational behaviour can be of inestimable value to a designer; it may not be easy for him to establish, or even to know, the exact conditions of operation if he decides to make his own tests; it may not even be possible.

By its very nature, operational testing means what it says—testing during productive operation. It is therefore quite wrong to estimate the costs by means which include those elements of the materials, equipment, running expenses, etc, which would in any case be included in the costs of normal operation. The only costs of operational testing are those incurred by instrumentation (instruments themselves, recording apparatus, and associated maintenance and calibration), where necessary, and *additional* to that in normal use, plus, of course, the *extra* labour costs involved in observing, recording, transmitting, and analysing the data required. To ignore this is to be faced with artificially high costs when, in fact, operational testing is normally by far the cheapest method of accumulating the most valuable design and development information.

Who should pay? In arriving at decisions as to the cost of monitoring operational behaviour, it may well be worth while to do a little investigation as to whether other parties—that is, other than the user himself— may be prepared to bear or share it. There are examples of the supplier agreeing to some such arrangement as the provision of a discount from the initial price in exchange for information—or for facilities to obtain it; his representative may wish to be present during the operations. He may be prepared to give some cost concession for the privilege of having defective, inadequate, or broken parts of an equipment returned to him so that a comprehensive examination can be made and the results used in modification and improvement—that is, development. When the supplier is not prepared to pay for these exchanges, it is still clearly to the user's advantage to help improve the equipment that he is using. Apart from gaining knowledge about the actual usage and how to optimise it, the intrinsic information may be of little use to him unless he is in proper communication with the supplier, who can usually advise both in regard to what constitutes significant data and also as to the necessary instrumentation or methods of monitoring.

Influence on each other of operating parameters. As for the supplier or manufacturer, testing to represent the real conditions of operation can rarely be done exactly. Even when the environment expected can be reproduced in the greatest detail, there is still the effect of the operator who may be more or less skilled than the manufacturer's design or testing staff, but who is unlikely to have the same knowledge of, or mental attitude to, the equipment of which, after all, he is a user not a maker. Without comprehensive facilities for reproducing the actual working conditions, the manufacturer has to perform his testing, if possible, in a manner as near to them as he can; this is not always satisfactory. He may, therefore, decide to increase the severity of testing or parts of tests by imposing criteria beyond those expected in practice. This will not always provide the right sort of information and it can be particularly deceptive when parameters of operation have influence on each other.

As an example of this, some textiles, notably cotton, increase in tensile strength with the absorption of moisture, up to a limit. If it is known that a product which involves cotton as a strength member may have to operate in damp conditions, always giving a certain level of mechanical performance, it would not be helpful to the manufacturer to test in wetter conditions than are expected in practice. His tests for tensile strength can produce results which mislead him into making assumptions that the product was adequately strong—when in fact the wetness had produced an artificially high value.

Buying operational information from users. Generally speaking, the manufacturer's amount of testing is small compared to the aggregate amount of operation which will be experienced by his products. It is also relatively much more costly. So he may well find that it is wasteful doing on a small scale what someone else is doing on a large scale and at lower (specific) cost. If this is the case, it could be a very profitable venture to take all steps, including direct payment, or indirect reward, by means of discounts or concessions of one kind or another, to collect usable information from routine operations. In particular, this service information is most valuable because, as is well known, the user is continually inventing ways of abusing the product in a manner not foreseen by the designer.

Of course, the co-operation between user and supplier in this provision of operational information requires considerable goodwill and understanding on the part of all those concerned. Improvement in design quality or reliability involve detective-like investigations in which clues have to be sought from a wide range of data, and cause and effect may have to be established. The overall problems are similar to jig-saw puzzles with no well-defined boundary lines, however, within which all the pieces fit. The evidence which must be rationalised and co-ordinated includes materials, design, manufacture, and use and, involved in all of these, is the human element. The latter is one of the most important contributions to difficulty in fitting the pieces together, since it is apt, even unintentionally, to distort the evidence. Hence, the importance of trying to eliminate subjective opinions and seeking the actual original values of operational parameters, *not* a clean copy of the dirty log sheet, *nor* a copy from which apparently *outré* results have been eliminated.

Testing for life. There are cases where life testing can be performed by the maker. Since life takes a lifetime to achieve and tests cannot be allowed to hold up sales, it is usual to have them proceeding in a continuous manner during normal commercial activities. In this form, tests are often important advertising and selling aids. A prospective customer can see for himself that his supplier is taking steps to assure him of suitability for purpose *and* reliability or economy. Any claims normally made in the course of advertising have tangible backing and can be further supported by the publication of relevant test results.

Test rigs. Test rigs being expensive, it is usually better to have simple, carefully thought-out rigs than more comprehensive ones. Where several properties or qualities have to be established it is often more economical to test each separately and simply, than to try to evolve a universal and complicated set-up. Multi-purpose machines are, in any case, rarely capable of being designed to provide full satisfaction for each purpose, and are, at best, a compromise.

Simulated failure tests are most valuable. If, as a result of information from operation or the return of broken parts, the method and conditions of failure can be established, rigs can be designed for testing in a manner which produces the same results. From these, the designer can learn a great deal about the weakest links in his chain of design, and take appropriate action to prevent or, at least, defer failures. Collaboration between user and designer is therefore particularly important in this instance.

What is meant by "life." In life testing it is sometimes found that the product concerned gradually falls in performance until such a time as it fails completely. Some products, on the other hand, continue with virtually full performance until the end of their lives, which is characterised by unexpected, or "catastrophic" failure. Beteween maker and user there must, therefore, be a clear understanding as to what is meant by "life." It might denote the time (or duration such as numbers of

105

cycles or operations) which elapses before the product is completely unable to operate at all; or it might be the time beyond which the performance has fallen below a prescribed or specified set of values. It might be acceptable to the user that, even after the specified level of performance can no longer be achieved, there is still some use in the product, albeit at a lower level or efficiency, which for some time, justifies continuing operation rather than incur the cost of replacement.

Considerations of this nature lead to the necessity for definitions of different aspects of "life" such as the following:

1 *Design life*. That expected life during the whole of which the performance complies in all respects with the conditions stipulated or specified.

2 *Useful life*. That expected life during the whole of which some useful performance can be derived.

3 *Total life*. That expected life from the beginning of use until complete failure.

The three definitions give an increasing order of magnitude of life.

It should be noted that the word "expected" appears in all these definitions, for they represent an agreed expectation between maker and user. Experience and feed of data from operation will move expectation nearer to actuality.

Accelerated life. The life of a product can sometimes be examined by testing in a manner which accelerates the end point, and so provides early information. This might otherwise take too long to be acceptable. It is usually done by increasing one or more parameters of test. For example, a machine running at 1000 rpm in normal operation could be tested at 1250 rpm; a component intended to withstand pulls of 50 tons could be tested at 75 tons; an electric radiator element designed to operate at 400 °C could be tested at 500 °C. The chief difficulties, in addition to the actual decisions about the change in parameters, are in the interpretation of the results.

Life patterns. Unless a great deal is known about the shape of the life curve—that is, how the product changes in behaviour in the course of time—the results of accelerated life tests must be treated with great reserve.

106

Linear life. If, for instance, the life in normal use is characterised by a smooth and uniform reduction in performance, this is said to be a linear life curve. Such a curve is common to products or components which come to the end of their lives as a result of uniform wear. An example is the lead in a propelling pencil. In these cases, interpretation of results of either accelerated or part life tests, can be made with reasonable accuracy and confidence, for if half the life (or length of pencil lead) is lost in a given time, it can be assumed that the whole life is likely to be twice that value. Alternatively, if in the use of the product in test, a means can be devised to increase the rate of wear to, say, twice the normal value—by doubling the pressure, the normal whole life could again be deduced as twice the test life, if indeed doubling the pressure doubled the wear rate. If, on the other hand, doubling the pressure increased the wear rate four-fold, a life test could be made in one-quarter of the actual duration, and so on.

All these methods are entirely dependent on knowing the life pattern, and also the effects, of the different parameters on this pattern. Unfortunately, very few products behave in a way which can be rationalised in this manner. In particular, those products which have lives characterised by catastrophic failure at the end, are almost impossible to handle by means of accelerated tests.

Catastrophic failure. It could be the case, for example, that the full performance was maintained until breaking point and no deduction could be made by normal testing over a shorter period, say half the expected life; for there might be no measurable change at that point. Again, the design may be so critical for a particular parameter that, attempting to shorten life by, say, the use of an increased imposed load, causes instant or quick failure. Similarly, a small reduction in the load might lead to a virtually indefinite life. In all these cases, no simple deductions can be made, and so-called accelerated life tests must be, at the least, suspect, and at the best, treated with extreme caution.

Nevertheless, accelerated life testing of one or other form *is* performed and can sometimes provide useful information about the method of failure. In most cases, however, it can only be treated confidently as a valuable means of *comparison* of lives, for if one product fails before another of a similar kind and in the same testing, it is most likely that it would also fail first in normal use. Used in this way and knowing the limitations, relatively crude accelerated life tests can be useful tools of development—which, as has been stated, requires the measurement of what is better, or what constitutes an improvement. But to measure actual values of life may require further careful consideration.

Testing to specification. Notwithstanding all that has been said previously about the over-riding value of testing in actual operation, the customer always requires some sort of assurance that what he intends to buy will act as expected. So, where it is not possible or sufficiently satisfactory to reproduce the working conditions on the manufacturer's premises, some other kind of demonstration of fitness for purpose is necessary. Where generations of products have resulted in the accumulation of a sufficiently large volume of operational data, he may be satisfied with evidence from that experience. On the other hand, and particularly in the case of a new or modified product where no such experience is available, it is necessary to require some degree of testing at the works of the manufacturer. In any case, the manufacturer will himself wish to take those measures which contribute to the control of quality, and which in the end maximise his profit by ensuring that what is produced satisfies his customers.

These measures are best written into a specification of the whole product, which, as indicated in Chapter 5, should include not only a clear description of all requisite quality attributes but also a description of the means whereby this quality can be demonstrated. Specification tests are, therefore, of two kinds; those ensuring that the right quality or aggregate of characteristics is embodied in the final product, and those aimed at proving that a product of this quality will perform as required. The first group is called property or characteristic tests and the second, performance tests. A clear line of demarcation is not always evident, especially for example, when the performance required is itself a static property—such as the withstanding of a certain force—or the resistance to a particular chemical effect.

Normally, the property tests are those which enable the manufacturer to maintain his control of quality by taking steps to see that all concerned at whatever level, are kept aware of what is going on. This may be achieved by the setting up of continuous (and preferably) pictorial records for each particular property, and operated as indicated in Chapter 3.

While it is preferable for property or performance tests to be representative of operational conditions, this is not always necessary provided that certain measures are observed. These are to ensure that the tests performed have a well-defined relationship with operational experience—that is, can be correlated. This relationship can apply to property tests which may be critical to performance, such as when a given tensile strength is equivalent to a certain life in use. This correlation is part of the procedure for the writing of specifications. The value of the ultimate specification depends on the extent to which its various requirements produce the desired effect, whether they mimic it or not. This is an important reason for keeping a specification under review. It ensures that the descriptions of attributes and tests, including methods and criteria of judgement, are adequate to produce a product which behaves as required. If not, or when it is desireable to modify the behaviour, it can provide the facts needed to adjust the descriptions.

Examples where correlation with practice are necessary include those in which otherwise the specification requirement would have to result in damage to the product, as for instance in the production of conveyor belting. It is obviously absurd to cut test samples from anywhere but the ends, in order to minimise damage. So the specification requirements which might involve a number of mechanical tests, besides other properties and physical dimensions, can only be representative of a small part of the end of perhaps several hundred feet of continuous product. However, the parameters of production such as temperature, pressure, speed of flow, might not have settled down to stability at the beginning of production and might also be affected by conditions at the end of the run. The result is that the ends may not be representative of the whole. Nevertheless, if tests on small samples, to fixed criteria of, for example, strength, correlate with satisfactory behaviour in service, the specification is adequate in regard to these tests. Specification tests, therefore, must be correlated with the corresponding effects in use, especially when they are not apparently representative of service conditions.

Specification test equipment

A specification which stipulates a datum of quality or performance must also include both the methods and the criteria for achieving this. Specification tests comprise:

1   A completely detailed description of the apparatus or equipment used.
2   The methods of use.
3   The criteria of passing or failing in terms of quality values, with tolerances where necessary and possible.

These three requirements—equipment, method, and criteria—need not necessarily be placed together in the specification. More often than not, the first two may have alternatives or can be stated in wide terms, provided that the necessary features are given in careful detail. It is usual, therefore, to indicate the quality level first, adding any other criteria such as tolerances, and, in separate sections, the equipment and methods (of both testing and recording).

This is very significant to development. Whether a manufacturer is already equipped or not to perform this work, when a customer purchases against a specification, it immediately becomes necessary for him (the manufacturer) to become so. The customer will require to know before purchasing, that the various stipulations agreed are capable of being assured by means of all the appropriate test equipment and facilities. Periodical checks by the customer or his representative, in the form of a visit to the factory premises, are usually made for the purpose of witnessing a demonstration in the form of specified tests. No other assurance is as satisfactory.

In many cases, especially when the customer is a large purchaser, he himself has all the facilities for checking for compliance with specifications, so it is even more important for the manufacturer to protect himself by ensuring that nothing is sold which is likely to be rejected.

Having installed this equipment, the manufacturer uses it as an important part of his procedures for controlling quality, in inspection, etc. It also becomes an important feature of his actual production process. The mere continual testing of different properties or other requirements will begin to throw up information which, when evaluated, will relate the various process steps to the quality level, and not merely provide uniformity. Such information, when passed to those concerned, sometimes enables processes to be tightened up and the working margins beyond the specification (*see Figure 8*) to be reduced, thus making production more economical. In general, however, the setting up of rational facilities for the controlling of compliance with a required standard, creates the very situation which leads automatically to improvements and development in this sense. The tools that are involved in the measurement of quality and which enable the manufacturer to fulfil his responsibility for quality, are also those which create development.

Destructive testing. Destructive testing is obviously extremely important when it is required to know accurately the condition of ultimate failure. No other type of testing is equally satisfactory for this purpose. It is valuable, as previously indicated (*see page 105*), when it can be performed in the manner in which failure takes place in practice. This is helped by information from usage and by the examination of failed equipment. Its chief value, however, is in the process of ensuring that the *capability* of the equipment is greater than its prescribed or expected *duty*.

In the case of machines or complex systems, it is also one way of ascertaining the areas in which failure is likely to take place. It is, by its nature, an expensive method of testing, but it is often well worth while even in cases of very high cost, especially when suitable arrangements can be made to limit the test in such a way that no further damage occurs after first failure. Thus, even in the case of, say, a very large turbo-generator that is intended to run continuously at a high and constant level of performance, it might be worth while to overload it on test (by higher speed, greater output, or other increase in parameters of operation) in order to find out what is its first weakness—what gives way first. Clearly, it would be an economic necessity to stop the test as quickly as possible on failure to find what had gone. It may not be easy to prevent further, almost instantaneous, damage, but if this can be done, most valuable data becomes available. Destructive testing should therefore be considered in the light of what is possible, what precautions can be taken to ensure the limiting of cost, and what may have to be done so as not to prejudice the safety of the whole procedure. The results, expensively obtained, can then be confidently used in the design of whole generations of costly machines.

Where destructive testing is the only possibility. It should be noted that there are some cases where *only* destructive testing has any significance at all. These are instances in which the performance or requirement is itself a destruction, as in the case of a match or an explosive charge. The only way to find out whether the performance is correct is to strike the match, or to explode the charge. There is, therefore, no sure way of testing the whole of production, or any particular part of it, except by rendering it useless. In these cases, destructive testing can only be performed on a small sample of production, selected by carefully chosen means and in consideration of the economics involved. Here great reliance has to be placed on the accuracy of the control of quality, taking all possible steps to ensure that each unit will probably behave in a way identical with that of the destroyed test sample.

Welding. There are many other examples in which destructive testing is the only satisfactory procedure to prove something. Some of these present special problems. Welding, for example, is a very important engineering process and one on which much might depend. One can make a destructive test on a welded joint and demonstrate, by measuring the effort required to destroy it, by the nature of the break, or by a visual inspection of the weld itself, that it was unsatisfactory. It is virtually impossible, however, to destroy a welded joint and prove it as having been satisfactory. So much depends on the welder himself, that obviously the first precautions required to ensure a sound weld are to see that he is well-trained, certificated, and kept up to date. He must also be provided with the right equipment and be able to work in the right conditions. (This is control of quality.) As a check, long test welds can be examined by taking a large number of cross sections. As a first approximation, it can be assumed that the variations from one section to another, in terms of consistency and strength, are likely to be similar to the variations which will occur from one weld to another. This provides a reasonable guide to the range of workmanship which can be accepted, but obviously, checks of a similar nature have to be made from time to time and nothing must preclude the examinations of welds by other means—for example, non-destructive testing and expert visual inspection.

Fatigue testing. More and more prominence is being given to fatigue testing. This is also destructive. Fatigue is one of the properties of materials which has not been given as much attention as it deserves. It is a property about which so little quantitative information has been available that it has been hoped to mask this with a "factor of safety" in design. It has virtually been ignored in specifications of materials.

Fatigue testing is a form of life testing (as is all destructive testing) in which "life" may be a number of cycles of stress changes, usually, but not always, reversals. Because of the inherent variations in materials due to their structure, it has been practicable, so far, only to consider orders of magnitude of numbers of cycles. For example, there is virtually no difference in life between samples which fail in the range two to four millions of stress changes; but they are unlike another set of samples failing in the range two hundred to four hundred millions of cycles. One order of magnitude may not be sufficient to indicate the possible variations in what appear otherwise to be identical materials.

Methods of expressing fatigue life must therefore be, for example,

112

logarithmic so that scales on graphs, etc, are capable of showing vast variations in numbers. Test results which indicate a wide scatter in which one value may be fifty or a hundred times another, must be accepted as the true state of affairs. No rounding off, or striking out far-out results must be done, for these are probably the most valuable results and pointers to failure in service hitherto unexplained.

Interpretation of fatigue tests. Since fatigue tests result in such a wide scatter, how can they be interpreted for the benefit of other parts of production? This is a very controversial question and has produced many suggestions. One, which appears to have some merit, is to make the tests into accelerated life tests by increasing the parameter of stress magnitude. The results are then interpreted in a way in which the *scatter* in fatigue life in the test is taken to be the likely scatter in fatigue life or strength in practice. In other words, a range of fifty to one in the accelerated tests can be assumed to point to a possible range of the same order in normal life. This enables top limits for strength to be used in the design processes, limits much lower than one might assume.

Valuable saving in time can be achieved by this type of testing, which can usually be performed on the most elementary of rigs. It can be supplemented by a few tests at the intended operating stress to determine the actual strengths on to which the range may be imposed. Obviously it has to be augmented, however, by continuous examination of equipment withdrawn from service and further research into fatigue properties.

Non-destructive testing. Destructive testing destroys; even other types of testing may affect that which is tested. So it is usually necessary to take small samples from the product or a small proportion of the actual products, for test purposes. It may, however, be required to make a complete check of a particularly important unit which is to go into service. The method of test must obviously not adversely affect the very property (or any other, for that matter) under examination. A non-destructive test has to be used.

Many types of non-destructive testing are available and have been described, but there are certain important features which are common to most. One of these features is the method of interpretation of the results. Clearly it is not possible to measure a breaking strength except by breaking something. From a non-breaking test, only a *deduction* can be made about the possible ultimate break. Therefore these tests are generally expensive not by virtue of the cost of the test equipment, but because of the requirement of highly skilled staff both to maintain and calibrate the equipment, and especially to interpret the results. These may have to be extrapolated, where required, with accuracy and, most importantly, with a high degree of confidence.

Ultrasonics. As a typical example of non-destruction testing, consider the use of ultrasonic equipment to locate possible internal flaws in an important component such as an axle, a boiler plate, or a girder. In very simple terms,this involves receiving an "echo" of ultra-sound from a discontinuity in the specimen to be examined. (The frequency of the ultra-sound is usually in the range between hundreds of thousands and millions of cycles a second, or from about twenty to two hundred times the frequency of audible sound in its top range.) The echo can be compared with those of, for example, the far side of the specimen, and any flaw can be located in space, and identified in shape and size. The chief difficulty is in the interpretation of the record which purports to give this information, and it requires considerable skill to provide answers with confidence. It is not always possible to indicate the significance of the flaw. A spherical inclusion of 1 mm or less in diameter in a thick plate may be of virtually no import, whereas an elongated streak of the same volume might be the cause of a subsequent crack.

The best way to achieve confident interpretation of a non-destructive test is by destruction; by breaking or opening up an occasional sample to check the deduction. If this is not possible, calibration tests on known flaws in deliberately made-up specimens should be performed before and after each substantive test. Thus, in the use of ultrasonic testing, the operator should provide himself with "equivalent" axles, plates, girders, etc, which are constructed with different types and sizes of flaw in known locations. Testing on actual production cases can then be directly compared with these.

Non-destructive testing should, therefore, have sources of comparison and, where possible, experience of destructive testing, in order that accurate deductions can be made.

114

Eight

Development II: Increase in Reliability

One of the improvements required of development is an increase in reliability. As more interest is arising in the subject, it will be found that customers will begin, generally at first, but then more specifically, to seek to purchase at a stated level of reliability. It is necessary, therefore, to examine various aspects of this subject.

Statistical view of reliability as a probability

We have earlier seen that there are many ways in which requirements of reliability can be defined. When these attempts are made, the supplier is faced with the problems of meeting the requirements and of eventually having to make claims about the reliability of his product. This poses certain difficulties. There are possible variations in the supply of his raw materials and components, however thoroughly controlled and examined. To these must be added different levels of performance of his designers, operators, and machines.

Whatever necessary steps he takes to achieve and check for consistency, he hopes that nothing was overlooked, nothing not thought of, and that nothing could intervene in the whole process, which could not possibly have been foreseen. His production processes, control routines, and tests have been arranged and put into practice in such a way that the required reliability has been aimed at to the best of his ability. Yet, this still leaves him with the fact that he can only indicate a probable outcome, however high the probability. His statement to the customer might be "I am 95 per cent sure that this product will behave in the manner you require and describe, for the stipulated length of time, provided it is used in the manner we have agreed between us." Alternatively, if more than one product is involved, he could say, "I am sure that no fewer than ninety-five of these 100 articles will behave. . . ." Without going into the attitude of the customer in the face of such a statement or claim, it can be seen that, as a generalisation, reliability can usually be expressed in the form of a probability. This concept, about which much has been written (*see*, for example, Richard E Barlow, *Mathematical Theory of Reliability*, Wiley, New York), is extremely useful in the latter case of numbers or continuous quantities of commodities, and, of course, it leads to greater accuracy as the numbers or quantities become greater. Thus, reliability, unlike quality, can be a simple number—a fraction always less than unity or a percentage less than 100. The probability of components performing as required for a given time and in given circumstances, when stated as 0.9995—that is, components with a reliability of 0.9995—simply means that, with all the available information from production and tests, the best guess that can be made with confidence about every batch of 2000 is that only about one failure need be expected.

The definitions of reliability which include statements of probability usually involve statistical methods during, or in parallel with, production and testing in order to measure the degree of confidence which can be placed in the results. This confidence is increased or improved when the numbers of equipment are larger. In the case of a single equipment such as a relatively complex machine, statistical methods can also be applied, using variations in the definitions of reliability to fit the circumstances. The requirement could be a reliability or probability of a certain magnitude "that the machine will be capable of operating within certain tolerance limits of a specified performance at any given instant of time in a particular period." Clearly, the methods of determination of the requirements of degree and nature of testing and measurement, will depend on the form of the definition chosen to establish the desired value of reliability.

In dealing with concepts of probability, it ought to be said in passing that engineers are sometimes understandably unreceptive. By virtue of their training and profession, they have a built-in tendency to show preferences for subjective evaluations rather than rely on probabilities, which to them are synonymous with calculated risks. For this reason, definitions in terms which imply somewhere a mathematical treatment of such ideas as degree of confidence, are only tolerated when they apply to very large numbers of data. This is a perfectly justifiable attitude which applies to many types of statistical presentation. Sometimes, it is considered more appropriate to set up activities on the basis of what appears to be another type of definition with no obvious statistical content—such as with single machines or complexes where, for example, the overall cost of their lifetimes may be required. Even then, however, the element of probability is inherently present, however disguised.

Attempts by prospective users at putting values to reliability are useful in encouraging designers to make an approach to the difficult problems which always arise in connection with reliability—and which, without this type of persuasion, might not otherwise be tackled. Unfortunately, the introduction of reliability into design fundamentals, has rarely been taught, and even in the case of development, the subject has, as yet, been treated relatively inadequately except for certain classes of product. These are in fact such things as mass produced electronic components, which lend themselves particularly to the statistical probability concepts, and which, by virtue of the ease of testing in numbers, provide results with a high degree of confidence.

With other requirements less easy to cater for, however, it is still important to make a choice of an appropriate definition in the light of the circumstances. However crude the final statement agreed, it will still be helpful in setting out the steps necessary to arrive at achievement. Its justification will be seen when the rough approaches become nearer the mark and more refined as experience is gained and fed into the system of communications.

Measurement of reliability

Testing for evaluation. Where by the nature of the product, which may be produced in large quantities notionally identical in quality, it is possible to conduct tests in numbers, the reliability is the proportion of success in attaining the test criteria. The degree of confidence with which this assumption is made depends on the weight of evidence. In general, it will be greater as the numbers of tests are greater, or will be increased by further confirmations. Statistical techniques are available to express this degree of confidence, which is also greater as the requirement of accuracy in the result is lower. For instance, the confidence in stating a reliability to be 0.9 ± 0.05, that is lying between 0.85 and 0.95, is considerably greater than the confidence in stating it to be 0.9 ± 0.01, or lying between 0.89 and 0.91.

Care has to be taken to ensure that the tests are not only identical, but also either directly comparable, or capable of being exactly correlated, with the actual conditions of usage. If the tests are made to specified requirements, however, these criteria should have been fulfilled during the finalising of the specification.

As an example of the type of product suitable for this method, consider lamp bulbs. These are designed for a life of 2000 hours when operated at a certain voltage and in a stated set of ambient conditions (temperature, humidity, air velocity, etc). They are tested in fairly large numbers and the reliability expressed as the number per cent which remain in use at the end of a 2000-hour test in these conditions. Slightly more complicated, further stipulations may be made as to "life," irrevocable failure not being the criterion. In this case, a minimum level of performance—for example, light output—is required. The light output would be monitored during the test, the criterion for reliability being modified to that proportion of bulbs remaining in use at the end of the 2000 hours with at least the minimum light output.

These methods are particularly suitable for small units such as electronic components used in systems in large numbers. It is in these fields that some of the most rapid advances have been made in the mathematical/statistical techniques for measuring reliability. The end result of testing is a value of reliability in the form of a probability which, however, has disadvantages to the potential user to the extent that it represents a calculated risk. Two defective units in a group of 100 tested, giving a reliability of 0.98, imply that the best guess one can make about the behaviour of the equipment in general is that in *every* 100 units there will be two defectives. It would not be exceptional to find no defectives in one group of 100 units, and four in another. Only further results and, better still, experience of behaviour in service, can give greater confidence in, and refine, this type of prediction which is based on the most usual definition of reliability—the probability of behaving as required under stated conditions, for a given time.

Reliability of systems

In order to discuss quantitative effects of reliability, it is useful to consider examples. Those following have been oversimplified in order to clarify argument. Suppose a machine consists of two parts only, called rotor and stator, and that the procedures for measuring reliability are a set of test routines to which numbers of each have been limited to six. It is found after the tests that for one reason or other, one rotor and one stator fail the tests. Without introducing degrees of confidence, the best guess one can make about the reliability of a product of which one in six has failed is that in any other set of six one might fail—that is, the reliability is five-sixths, or 0.833. Thus, the rotors and stators produced have reliability values of this magnitude. In the assembly of machines, obviously any rotor might be assembled with any stator and a machine is considered defective if either or both parts are defective. To find the reliability of the assembly, therefore, the sets of six of each component are joined together in all possible ways, each stator in turn with each rotor.

Suppose the defective stator were number 3 of the six and the defective rotor number 5, the results of making all possible combinations are shown in Figure 10, in which defective parts are shaded

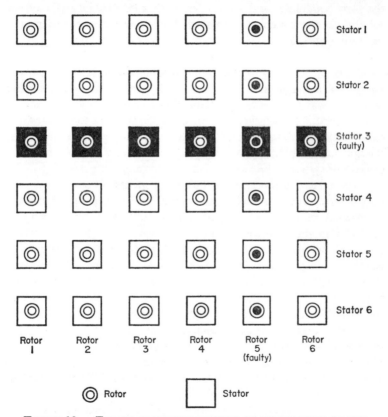

FIGURE 10   EFFECT OF THE RELIABILITY OF COMPONENTS ON THE RELIABILITY OF AN ASSEMBLY

If 5 out of 6 stators and 5 out of 6 rotors are reliable, then only 25 out of 36 assemblies of stator and rotor are reliable.

black. It will be seen that of the thirty-six possible combinations—that is, 6×6—eleven machines are defective in having one or both components faulty. The reliability of the machine is therefore 25/36 or 0.694,—that is, in every thirty-six assemblies, eleven failures may be expected.

It will be seen also that $25/36 = 5/6 \times 5/6$ and that the reliability of the assembly is the product of the individual reliabilities of the components.

From this type of examination, it can therefore be stated that, on the assumption that any component failure will produce a defective assembly or system, the reliability of the system is the product of all the unit reliabilities and always less than the reliability of any one. Accent was thrown on to system reliabilities by failure experienced in the early stages of the United States missile programmes.

Systems of large number of components. Although great care was taken in design and the highest skill brought to bear in manufacture, it was still found that failures were excessive and money not so well spent. The failures were, of course, largely due to the enormous complexity and numbers of components in the various systems. Although the reliability of each was high, their very number made the chances of system failure somewhere, sometime, quite high.

If the system comprised 100 000 components or units (and some missile systems have several times this number), a reliability of each and every component of 0.9999—that is to say that only one in every ten thousand might fail—could lead to the chance of successful accomplishment being only one in ten. A unit of a system need not necessarily be only a component, for the failure of a soldered joint, for example, would be equally undesirable. In this context, component A soldered to component B would provide three units in which reliability has to be considered—A, B, and the joint A-B. The expenditure of vast amounts of money on these ventures demands a reasonably high probability of success. If this were, say, 95 per cent or about nineteen successes out of every twenty attempts, the unit reliabilities, assuming them to be identical for simplicity, would have to be about 0.999 999 5, or only one expected failure in every two millions.

Of course, the assumption of equal reliability of each unit is a gross oversimplification for the sake of illustration. Nevertheless, it tends to show the necessity for requiring extremely high reliabilities in each unit in order that a complex system may be effective. When these necessities are placed before suppliers, encouragement is given to means whereby they are ultimately achieved.

On the other hand, there is an important consideration which must be examined in all cases of the requirement of high reliability of units in order to provide an acceptable overall system reliability. Sometimes this cannot be achieved except at great cost. So it is necessary to examine the system as a whole, including the scheme into which it may fit, and reduce it into sections each as simple as possible. In particular, these should be as independent of each other as possible so as to reduce the cumulative effects. The simpler each section, the less costly it is to achieve greater reliability, and so it is vitally important never to use, for example, an electronics system if the particular job can be done with a nut and bolt—metaphorically speaking.

Important elements in a complex system

Some units of a system are virtually 100 per cent reliable (a body casting, or a foundation plate). Some are more vital than others from the aspect of failure of the system. In the case of a vacuum cleaner the repair man who comes to the house to replace a driving band or a failed bearing might be able to show from his records (and those accumulated from his colleagues) that, in all the servicing of this model, only about half a dozen units gave any trouble during the reasonable life of the machine. Of these, four caused complete failure and two permitted machine operations of a kind—that is, noisy and requiring more effort. Some parts, the body or the handle, have never been known to require replacement. His ultimate advice might be to substitute a new driving band every three or four months and a new bearing once a year.

The accumulation of information about defects from actual operation has shown that, in this machine comprising a hundred components or units, ninety-four were as near to 100 per cent reliable as made no difference and six were sources of probable failures within a year. Their reliabilities, judged from tests and records, were successively:

> 1 failure in 10
> 1 failure in 5
> 1 failure in 10
> 3 failures in 10
> 1 failure in 10
> 1 failure in 20

Thus, the reliability of the whole system, in relation to, say, a year of operation, would be the product of the reliabilities of all the hundred parts of which only six were measurably less than unity. This would be, therefore:

$$1 \times 1 \times 1 \times \ldots (94 \text{ times}) \times 0.9 \times 0.8 \times 0.9 \times 0.7 \times 0.9 \times 0.95 = 0.388,$$

which would explain—and indeed forecast—two or three failures a year.

The most complex systems can be treated in the same way. A system composed of 100 000 units might have required attention to only about half a dozen, and the reliability would be:

$$1 \times 1 \times 1 \times \ldots (99\,994 \text{ times}) \times 0.99 \times 0.95 \times \ldots.$$

Design examination and the feed of operating data focuses attention on the important elements of a system. Analysis of defects or failures pinpoints the troubles and leads to their elimination or reduction. In the case of the vacuum cleaner, while the original design was unexceptionable from the aspects of mechanical strength, which was carefully calculated and checked, perhaps the possibility of a driving band perishing as a result of storage in a warm kitchen cupboard, had been overlooked.

Concentration of attention on the few important elements—important from the point of view of unreliability, not performance—enables finite resources to be economically applied to design improvements which might be intrinsically trivial, yet have a considerable effect on a system.

Stand-by design

Where the reliability requirements are critical it may be necessary to duplicate vital components of a system in a "stand-by" technique. This method is often adopted to increase reliability, the controlling factors being the cost of the additional equipment, space required, etc, considered in the light of the cost of the gain in overall reliability by direct design. Calculation of the gain in reliability can best be done on the basis of unreliability. Suppose a component with a reliability of 0.9 is to be duplicated. The unreliability is the complement of this—that is, 0.1. Assuming that the system is in satisfactory operation, if both or either of the duplicated components are working correctly, it will be seen that the probability of both failing is 0.1×0.1 or 0.01. The system reliability (assuming this is the only consideration) has therefore been increased to 0.99 by this duplication. Clearly, this is a useful design process, especially when it may not be possible—or prohibitively expensive—to provide a single component of reliability 0.99. For overall calculations of the reliability of the system, the duplication can be considered as the equivalent of the provision of this improved single component.

Obviously, this type of treatment in design can be extended and multiplied to achieve a required reliability. Three components in parallel and having reliabilities of only 0.8 each, would provide the equivalent of a single unit of reliability 0.992, since the unreliability has been reduced to $0.2 \times 0.2 \times 0.2 = 0.008$.

In considering systems, therefore, reliabilities are multiplied together when units are in series; whereas unreliabilities are multiplied together when units are in parallel.

Reliability of "one-off" equipment

Reliability is just as important for a single large or complex equipment as for a number of simple units. If it is a manufacturer's business to make one ship or a 200-megawatt turbo-generator every two years, it is vital to his future success that they are reliable. It is therefore necessary for him to learn everything he can about his product. This can best be achieved by carefully planned testing and by rational accumulation of operational experience from the same, or previous, generations of equipment. (*See Chapter 7.*)

Obviously, as with systems, the reliability of individual components is examined and special attention given to important elements. Where it is possible to foresee and evaluate a requirement of reliability in any one part or sub-assembly, this should be demanded of the relevant designers. Means will then have to be agreed to establish this value, or at least aim for it and review and adjust as necessary.

The ultimate performance requirements of machine or complex having been specified, it is important to attempt to predict its long-term behaviour—that is reliability—in numerical terms or otherwise. This attempt in itself will reveal needs for physical tests to establish those criteria—for example, of wear or deterioration—without which the prediction is too coarse. All this testing should be planned to provide the maximum amount of *useful* information for the least cost of testing. This is particularly important where there may be interactions between the effects of different parameters.

A machine with a well-defined pattern of behaviour under varying ambient temperature conditions, and another pattern under variations in humidity, may not, in a hot, wet climate, behave as might be predicted from the two individual effects. There is a large amount of published work available for reference in this field. Guidance can be obtained as to the proper considerations necessary for the effects of variation in behaviour under differing environmental conditions. [For example: *Increasing the Efficiency of Development Testing*, Pratt and Whitney Aircraft Corporation, East Hartford Connecticut, USA: lecture on film and publication.] In addition, the effects of the behaviour of individual components on the performance of a whole system or machine can be isolated.

Use of operational data to increase reliability

Where measurements of reliability are required from systems not amenable to test, or where testing would be uneconomic in satisfactory conditions, data must obviously be taken from operation. The proper communications and organisation are most important. They must be such that the feed of information from operation goes through a series of processes which result in the ultimate improvement of that operation. Such a system, as described elsewhere (*see Figure 2, page 22*), is a typical arrangement. Information is rationalised and prepared in a suitable form, and then made available to all concerned, but especially to those responsible for the subsequent action—for example, redesign —which will improve the system. The continuous accumulation of data in this way serves not only to help to predict the behaviour of machines, but also gradually to establish an increasing standard of behaviour. In other words, it is almost invariably true that any steps taken to quantify behaviour, to measure what is actually happening, to assess costs, lead automatically to improvement.

Principal factors which affect reliability

Designed or claimed values of reliability relate by definition, to an assumed set of operating conditions, environment, inter-action with other parts of a system. These must be unambiguously known to both supplier and user. The latter has to accept that the value achieved by design and intensive development can be reduced or increased—by utilisation in a different set of circumstances. Hence, the necessity for

124

close collaboration between both parties in arriving at reliability requirements.

Most statements of reliability, by definition, include also some time stipulation—for obviously the value required or claimed cannot be expected to maintain indefinitely. It is especially useful in cases where continuous operation is required, to quantify time aspects in relation to "outages" (failures to maintain operation) by the use of such parameters as "mean time between failures." These can be built into operating plans. In some cases, however, this type of concept is inapplicable and may even confuse the identification of the real causes of unreliability. Careful consideration must then be given to the significance of length of continuous operating time and to the possibility that, in particular uses, other measurements of "life" or "duration" such as the shape, magnitude and numbers of cyclical operations, may be more critical.

Everyday factors. In order to rationalise reliability, a great deal of attention has been given to complex problems arising from some of the above definitions or starting points. Not enough is paid to the simple everyday problems that everyone has known about for a long time and that will always continue to require consideration.

These include the effects of wear, vibration, shock, fatigue, humidity, corrosion, leakage, and the shape of time cycles, on "availability," or what is sometimes called "operational integrity." Some of these effects can be taken into account in terms of environmental conditions specified. Others cannot or may be superimposed on the assumed conditions. A watch wound every morning will run nicely and can be considered to have a high measure of reliability. The same watch wound only once a month, and allowed to run down in between, will give less confidence of availability for reliable operation. The same principle applies in the case of a car which can confidently be expected to start five or six times a day in more or less regular use. Less confidence will be felt if a start is attempted only once a month.

Any machine or system expected to remain inactive for lengthy periods—and yet be instantly available at full performance at any chosen time—would provide the designer with very severe design criteria to achieve a given reliability. This would be bound up with environmental effects while *not* in operation—such as corrosion, leakage, starting friction, fuel evaporation, loss of lubrication, battery discharge and other chemical effects, settling of dust or dirt, or ageing.

The reliability of such a system can be made high as a result of a development programme with carefully planned performance tests. However, this would only be possible if these everyday, non-operational, influences had been given first consideration.

Direct causes of unreliability

For any equipment, the chief causes of unreliability, however, are usually:

1   Design inadequacy.
2   Defects in manufacture.
3   Incidence of operating conditions beyond the design assumptions.
4   Effects of alternatives to reliability.
5   Relation of reliability to procedures.

None of these factors has a time relationship. This may explain the intensive resistance of engineers to definitions of reliability stipulating time. It will also be seen that most of these factors are largely bound up with defective quality in one form or other.

Design inadequacy. Quality and reliability start with design. The implications of the word "design" are not often completely understood and the usual context can be a mere skeleton of the overall picture which should be involved. "Design" is imagination. Arguments for and against (merely) drawing as a medium or language of engineering design, for example, are rather futile. Some designers need no drawings, some can manage with simple sketches, some cannot raise their imaginations from the two dimensions of a drawing or plan to the three of the ultimate product. It would be difficult to agree, on the basis of a flat drawing alone, the fitting-out with all its equipment, piping, valves, and so on, of an engine room of a battleship, or a congested part of a power station. Models may be required here.

If design is imagination, one test of their worth would be the study of the different results of a single design exercise performed by several designers who had been taught at the same time. Would the results be identical in achieving the original intentions? If so, what was taught was a formal process of a very narrow character and not the broader aspects of design. This is, unfortunately, what often occurs in practice. The dictionaries give definitions of design as:

1 A plan, scheme, project.
2 A preliminary conception of an idea, a delineation.
3 A purpose, aim, intention.

If the user specifies a set of requirements, it is inadequate to create a design by the usual concept of a delineation or drawing, without giving careful attention to the implications of 3. Unfortunately design is often taught for 1 and 2, and the inclusion of aspects of 3 taken for granted as requiring special personal characteristics in the designer.

The wider requirements of design to fulfil a specific purpose should be recognised as involving many aspects omitted from formal training. These include:

1 Ease of manufacture, rate of manufacture, and whether this works to the detriment of the user's purpose or not.
2 Requirements of life, safety, ease and economy of maintenance, ease of access and repair, ease and efficacy of lubrication, the elimination of requirements of lubrication, and the use of non-lubricable components.
3 Possible effects of handling, packaging, storing, the relation of the equipment to the user, the possible effects of installation and assembly, and the possible effects of abuse.
4 Effects of environment on equipment and *vice versa*, relation to other parts of a system if applicable.
5 The use of standard or well-tried components and sub-assemblies; the possible use of new materials, or the proper or better use of existing materials.
6 The intrinsic variability in critical materials and important elements; the possible effects of fatigue, corrosion, wear, shock, vibration, humidity, foreign matter, or dirt, etc.
7 Aesthetic considerations—functional veracity and pleasing the eye are not incompatible.
8 Inspectability, or the ability to check that what has been made is indeed fit for the purpose intended. It is a means of ensuring compliance by measurement and/or testing, with stipulated requirements of the user or with those attributes set down by the designer to fulfil them.

Those who design, therefore, have to make their minds and imagination alive to the existence of all these, and many more, aspects of design, which appear not be to connected with the technical process. They must learn to ask themselves the necessary questions. It follows that, having proved a design satisfactory from the simple technical point of view of the requisite performance, it has still to be re-examined, possibly component by component, from a production economics point of view. A slight change in design, for example, might make possible the use of interchangeable or standardised parts; a sense of cost reduction, essential in much successful design procedure, might lead to greater value for money; a knowledge of available materials could prove time saving, and the processes and ease by which they can be worked or machined, have a substantial effect on productivity.

A designer must be thoroughly conversant with manufacturing techniques, some of which may appear to be deceptively simple and, therefore, may be taken for granted, when in fact they need careful control. He must have in mind, when considering fitness for purpose, adaptability towards the operator and the environment, that a reasonable amount of abuse may have to be withstood. He might prefer either to design his equipment to be relatively insensitive to the effects of dirt and foreign matter, or, better still, to arrange to keep dirt out.

It is important to know the variation in quality of raw materials and to allow an appropriate margin in the design. So-called "factors of safety" are usually considerably less than assumed. This is due to inherent variations in materials and manufacture, on the one hand, and lack of knowledge of the worst possible working or operating conditions on the other. To improve reliability it is important to learn all one can about these areas of ignorance. Fatigue effects are becoming better known as a result of accumulation of test experience; in some cases it may be necessary to allow for a scatter of 50–100:1 in the number of reversals or changes of stress or loading which can cause failure in two apparently identical units of production. Thus, estimates of "life" can be seriously wide of the mark unless all such factors are considered in the light of the best knowledge available.

Reliability can be increased at the design stage by including a duplication of vulnerable parts in a stand-by technique as indicated previously, but this approach requires examinations of economic as well as physical possibilities—the former measured against the cost of outages or loss of production or continuous performance.

The user should allow the designer all necessary facilities to see and measure what is really wanted. This direct contact and the ultimate return of any defective parts to the designer are most important contributions towards the achievement of reliability. The man who designs equipment wants to see the broken pieces. If it is possible, he will then ask what were the true and accurate environmental and usage factors, as well as what he expects from both trials and tests in his own organisation and also field operation or simple user experience.

Finally, he must arrive at cost estimates of the achievement of different levels of reliability. For it must be clear to both parties that reliability costs money.

Defects in manufacture. The avoidance of defects in manufacture is a matter of control in the widest sense. The aim is compliance with the design requirements and the specified levels of the various "qualities" or attributes. The whole series of processes which can be (or ought to be) included under the title "manufacture" must be made *capable* of producing 100 per cent good articles. Thus, all steps taken, from raw material testing to that of the final product, must make the ultimate inspection a check, not a sorting or corrective procedure.

Reliability attainment in manufacture has tended to be confused with quality control and this latter, in turn, with inspection. The reason for this is not hard to find, since actual production is successful in so far as it results in compliance with the requirements. But those responsible, while aware of their key role in fulfilling these, must also be alive to the fact that this is but one step in the achievement of reliability.

Incidence of operating conditions beyond design assumptions. These may have taken place because of lack of sufficient knowledge for design, or because the conditions have changed from those assumed in first setting down design criteria, or simply because they are new and have never occurred, or been anticipated, before. In many cases, however, operating conditions beyond those assumed at the beginning occur because operators or users *invent* new uses or impose higher loads not visualised by the designer. The effects on reliability can, of course, be either up or down. The ultimate achievement may be greater or less than that expected. Steps must be taken to lead towards improvement rather than otherwise. These are not only the amelioration of the operating conditions, but also recording of what actually takes place and feeding this back to the designer in uncorrected form. No attempt should be made to allow for, or exclude, wide-of-the-mark results, since the odd exception may also be the cause of an unexplained failure; all "roughage" in the recorded values must be preserved.

Effects of alternatives to reliability. When dealing with reliability, it is necessary to consider alternatives which can have at least as important an effect on performance as the intrinsic value of reliability itself. While the latter may be a technical concept fixed by design and common to all subsequent production, the reliability experienced in use will obviously vary from one user to another. This arises from the possibility of departing from the conditions of use assumed in the original design, and also in such factors as kinds of supply, process, and installation, which may be peculiar to each customer.

Since the level of reliability is usually an economic question, it is often necessary to consider the alternatives available towards achieving the same ends. For it must be stressed that reliability costs money and the extent of reliability in the ultimate usage depends very substantially on what one is prepared to pay for it. Just as "stand-by" techniques can be used in design to create the effect of greater unit reliability, so alternative measures can be used *instead of reliability* (to some degree) as better economy.

At the commencement of any project, a decision is made on the minimum value of reliability which will achieve the required purpose; this can be as low as 60 per cent. The next step is to consider whether or not an increase in reliability would produce worth-while gains. If so, it might be achieved economically by adjustment of the environmental and operating conditions. The advice of the designer should be sought here, since in designing for a certain reliability he may have assumed pessimistically poor conditions of operation, a dirty atmosphere, or some operator abuse. More acute training, better lighting, a cleaner atmosphere, etc, may cost less than the advantages brought by the higher value of reliability.

If, however, a desirable increase in reliability is expensive, it might be cheaper, and yet achieve the same results, to provide more frequent maintenance. This can sometimes be scheduled conveniently at non-operating times.

A design in unit sub-assembly construction, which permits easy and quick substitution of defective sections of the system, might also be cheaper in the long run than the cost of a higher reliability.

These, and other suitable alternatives for high intrinsic reliability, obviously require the necessary attention to supporting arrangements.

Spares and facilities have to be available in the right quantities, at the right places, and at the right time. It is then no use, having provided these, if the men needed to do the job—usually not a full time occupation—are somewhere else and not readily available at the time.

Relation of reliability to procedures. Factors coming under this heading are parallel with those in the preceding section since they may over-ride, or substitute for, intrinsic reliability in equipment. The relation of the equipment to the other parts of the system has been mentioned. In addition to associated parts, however, services, operators, and procedures have to be considered. To optimise the reliability of systems as a whole (which includes not only the concrete bits and pieces), studies other than simple engineering, have to be made. Some of them are in the nature of probability games such as:

1   Whether the policy of substitution of components in a system should be by time of service, at certain specified periods, or merely at actual breakdown. The controlling parameter could be the magnitude of the costs of failure during operation, having regard to consequentials.

2   How is the effectiveness (or availability at an accepted performance level) of the system, over a stipulated life, dependent on the numbers of spare parts provided?

3   What is the optimum maintenance policy and schedule (frequency), so that the total costs of breakdown, operational losses, etc, *plus* maintenance and spares, are a minimum? (Obviously, too little spent on maintenance may involve unacceptably high operational losses and costs: too much will make the maintenance bill unnecessarily high.)

4   The determination of an inspection policy in cases where it requires inspection to discover defects or failures, having regard to the minimum total of the costs of preventative measures of this nature plus those of the failures.

5   The economics of designing redundancy into the system, having regard to the cost of this procedure and the cost of lower reliability. This is the "stand-by" technique discussed previously.

All these problems of optimum procedure are studies of probability. They are usually examined by the application of special mathematical techniques. As is the case with other factors affecting reliability, they need data to digest, and they are only successful in so far as the organisation for the provision of operational information is successful. This must feed the rational data, and then ensure that the results of these analyses are applied back to the operating systems.

In general, therefore, factors affecting the reliability of equipment are relatively simple to state although, in many cases, possibly extremely difficult to evaluate accurately. They certainly require the right atmosphere, organisation, and mentality in making any sort of successful approach and they have one thing in common. Attempts at knowing what is going on quantitatively, are virtually identical to those required to promote development. If one were asked to generalise or to make a simple statement covering the whole field of development and reliability, one could do no better than quote:

> "The engineering procedure for developing a product which will not fail in service does not require a mathematical definition of reliability. It does, however, require a precise knowledge of two items; the operating conditions and the strength of the device." (John De S Coutinho: reliability Director, Lunar Excursion Module of Apollo, Grumman Aircraft Engineering Corporation, New York.)

Nine

Purchase of Quality

The problems facing an intending purchaser are many, and vary in complexity according to circumstances, but apart from the obvious requirement of getting best value for money, two are of especial significance in the purchase of quality. These are the choice of the correct purchase from a range of possibilities, and the maintenance of, or increase in quality, in both that case and, more especially, when the choice is restricted. Everyone has faced the first problem at one time or another—what to purchase from a number of products with different prices corresponding to several qualities. It is worth while attempting to rationalise this situation, to present it in an organised manner which can then be a basis for adopting possible procedures of an optimum character.

How to choose from a range of qualities

You get what you pay for. Some generalisations can be stated first in order to provide a framework. For instance, one is that "you get what you pay for"—inelegant but expressive! Roughly, this means that you cannot expect to buy high quality except for a high price; conversely, the expenditure of little money usually purchases low quality. What seems to be implicit in these statements, however, is that you buy equal quality for equal money; that for x quality you pay money mx, and for z quality you pay mz, and so on. If this were exactly the case, purchasing procedures would be considerably simplified. There would be no bargains, no best buys. The choice would be determined simply by the quality required, expressed in any terms, such as length of useful life. The main consideration would be the choosing of an expeditious or convenient time at which a renewal or

133

replacement should take place—and then purchasing accordingly. The price for each unit of quality would be constant.

This state of affairs rarely exists. Usually, for a relatively small change in price, vast changes in quality are available; sometimes a range of qualities is available for approximately the same price, and so on. So the original generalisation is not quite true. It would appear that a useful parameter to examine would be the price per unit of quality. This immediately raises the problem of measurement of quality, for it is usually the case that the level of quality is neither indicated nor easily isolated.

Experience can of course provide information as, for example, with useful life. Let us suppose that there is a range of articles of which it is proposed to examine three. These cost £5, £6, and £10 respectively and, with the usual generalisation above, are expected to provide increasing life with price. In fact, this is generally the case, for experience has shown that the lives are, on average, about 15 000, 20 000, and 25 000 hours, showing that the more you pay, the more you get.

When these are examined by means of the criterion of price per unit life, however, a different picture emerges, for the values are 6s 8d (£0.33½), 6s (£0.30), and 8s (£0.40) for each thousand hours respectively, showing that the best value for money is the middle choice. Of course, there are other considerations determining what is actually purchased, such as the simple fact that only £5 is available, or that only 10 000 hours are required, or that after-sales service is better or worse in one case than another. But this trivial example illustrates that while high quality usually demands high price, you do not always "get what you pay for."

To take this further, it can be said that commodities in which a range of qualities can be purchased obey a law similar in shape to that shown in Figure 11. Taking an abscissa of an arbitrary range in increasing order of quality and an ordinate representing the value of those qualities, a curve *OAB* can be drawn. It is usual to find that it is impossible to achieve ideal (or 100 per cent) quality, so the curve is asymptotic to the ideal, approaching it nearer and nearer but never actually attaining it. In this consideration, quality is shown as that which is required—that is, a desirability of some kind, life, performance, safety, etc. The second ordinate is one of cost, and the curve *OCD* represents the cost of each quality, and shows that, the nearer to the ideal, the higher the increase in cost. That is, the cost of a given quality *increase* is low at low qualities and high at high qualities. The value

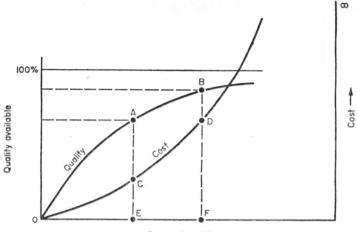

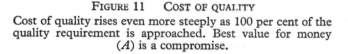

FIGURE 11   COST OF QUALITY

Cost of quality rises even more steeply as 100 per cent of the
quality requirement is approached. Best value for money
(*A*) is a compromise.

obtained for money at quality *A* may be represented by the ratio *AE/CE*
in some acceptable units, and that at quality *B* by *BF/DF*. Alternatively,
the price per unit quality at each of these is the reciprocal, *CE/AE* or
DF/BF.

If one could draw such curves accurately (these are merely illustra-
tive), these ratios would be helpful in determining best value for money
or least price per unit quality. If, however, it were absolutely necessary
to have a certain quality—for example, for safety reasons—then the
price to be paid might be virtually fixed and this would not necessarily
represent best value for money.

Price per unit of quality

From simple basic considerations, the next step is to consider directly
these ratios, which are more important than the elementary parameters.
Price per unit quality should be of more interest to the purchaser than
price. The range of qualities provides the situation shown in Figure 12,
where the price per unit quantity in any scale of measurement such
as length, area, volume, weight, or numbers (or simply the "price")
is plotted against the price per unit quality; quality having the same
criteria as indicated above, namely, life, performance, safety, etc.

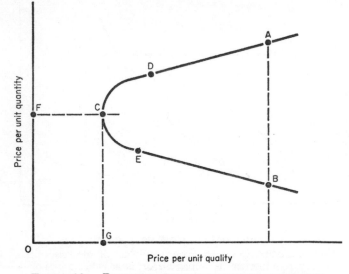

FIGURE 12   PRICE BEHAVIOUR IN RELATION TO QUALITY

The same value for money can be obtained by paying
a high price for high quality or a low price for low
quality. The purchaser's object is to locate (C) the point
of the best bargain.

A represents a high quality for which a high price has to be paid;
B, a low quality purchased for a low price. Both of these can be identical
in terms of price per unit quality, just as a £5 article giving 15 000
hours of life and a £10 article giving 30 000 hours of life, are identical
in the same terms. Somewhere in between qualities *A* and *B* may be a
quality *C* with a better value for money or lower price per unit quality—
for example, £7 for 25 000 hours of life.

This curve is an over-simplification in the extreme, for in nearly all
real cases where it can be quantified, *C* is not a point but an ill-defined
region and the curve itself is a crude band rather than a line. Furthermore, there are usually many considerations, other than the simple
ratio, which might be over-riding factors in purchasing procedures—
after-sales service, connection with other purchases from the same
source, etc. It is only rarely possible to construct this curve for a range
of commodities for the reason described earlier, namely, lack of information of a quantitative nature on the actual qualities. Nevertheless, the
situation portrayed is recognisable and can be said to obtain generally,

since even very high prices can barely buy ideal quality, whereas very low prices are virtually certain to buy low quality—showing that somewhere there are two prices at which the price per unit quality is the same.

A curve of this type is of such value that, wherever possible and especially in case of continuing supply requirements, as much information as possible on quality should be sought from all sources (but particularly from operation), in order to fill in the gaps and reduce the first roughness of any attempt at constructing such a curve.

It is often said that competition causes prices to tend towards value for money and that in the right atmosphere of activities between purchasers and would-be suppliers, rationalisations of this nature are so much trouble that it is not worth while making attempts to achieve them. In fact, however, purchasing pressures and the competition for what may be substantial orders, tend always to drive prices *down*, not necessarily towards lowest price per unit quality. This would be acceptable if purchasing had hitherto taken place at a quality higher than optimum represented by point D, where such price reductions would cause a move towards quality C and, in fact, better value for money. It would not be acceptable, however, if purchasing had been at quality E, lower than optimum, and reductions in price moved the situation in the direction of B rather than C. Competition is good if one is actually paying too much for quality, but bad if one is paying too little.

The move from E towards B occurs as a result of many reasons, most of which arise when the orders are big and it is vital to remain or become a supplier. Thus, quality may be lowered or jeopardised by the introduction (where not fixed by specification) of cheaper materials and methods, the cutting of production costs, the reduction in wrongly so-called non-productive activities such as research, development, and control of quality. Where criteria are fixed by specification, the lowering of margins of tolerance or the tightening of production control limits, may be methods by which the production costs are reduced, but all such activities tend to make non-compliance more likely (and usually rebound by requiring more acute inspection, and so on, *if* the customer is vigilant in his own interests).

For the purchaser, therefore, it is important to try to recognise the part of the curve at which commercial activities are taking place. This is very difficult but some help can be obtained from his technical colleagues or the actual users. They may at least know the quality being purchased is not good enough or, alternatively, too good for the job in hand. Should the position be recognised as at *E*—that is, that the quality may be too low—the most advantageous procedure would be to seek a higher quality and pay a higher price. Where a higher quality is not immediately available, suppliers should be encouraged to aim at this by development, by the imposition of tighter controls in production, by the use of better materials, etc, all of which increase cost, a fact of life which must be recognised by the purchaser.

In the absence of means of absolute measurement of quality, it is possible to devise relative methods similar to the first approaches to the differential calculus, where the effects of making small changes must be measured. Thus, if a slightly higher price brings an increase in quality greater than might be expected from the current price per unit quality, the situation is as at *E* and the procedure can be continued with a further increase after sufficient experience has been obtained. In the case of large purchases this need only be done initially over a small part of the total, provided that the results are observed carefully. If it is suspected that too high a price is being paid, the purchase of a slightly cheaper commodity (again over a small part of the total) should be used to measure the decrease in quality, which should be less proportionately than the price decrease would seem to indicate. This is the situation at *D*.

All these methods are easier to describe than to put into operation, and none are so clear cut as the idealised picture above. Nevertheless, attempts have to be made to optimise purchasing. Pressure must be put on users to provide quantitative evidence as to quality and advice as to levels required, and all this evidence collected together to fill in as much of the picture as possible. This is a difficult process in sporadic purchasing of odd commodities, but less difficult with the regular purchasing of large quantities of a commodity about which a great deal of experience can be accumulated.

Purchasing to specification

While it is highly desirable to be able to purchase on a quality basis—that is, purchase as a result of considerations additional to first cost—it is sometimes the case that purchasing purely in terms of best value for money nevertheless provides too low a quality for the user's purpose. This was briefly dealt with on page 135 in relation to Figure 11 which referred to the example of safety. In this case, a stipulation, preferably in the form of a specification of minimum requirements, must be made; price may be secondary. Buying rubbish extremely cheaply can be demonstrably good value for money if one only measures it by the criterion of price per unit quality.

In fairness to purchasers generally, it is their duty to get the best bargain possible, so it is always necessary to provide rationalised advice from the users as in the case of competitive purchasing from a range of qualities. The most helpful advice that can be provided is that which restricts the range; one example is the setting of minimum requirements.

The best advice of all, however, is a completely comprehensive specification rigorously fixing a single overall quality. Here the consideration is one of price only. The supplier with the lowest production costs can provide the best bargain or the lowest price per (fixed) quality. On the assumption that all products submitted are identical in respect of compliance with specification, the best buy is the cheapest.

Because a fully comprehensive specification is rarely provided, however, and since most are in the form of presenting minimum requirements, the purchaser often tends to seek reasons beyond the specification for different prices for apparently the same product. Similarly, when more than one product is offered at the same price, he looks at the additional properties not specified, or the margin by which the minimum requirements specified are exceeded. This is normally a bad practice. Where, for example, a single measured attribute, for example, tensile strength, is consistently higher than the specified minimum value, on no account should this be used by the purchaser to, in effect, pit one supplier against another as providing something for nothing, or a little extra. To favour such an offer with the order would merely cause a competition between intending suppliers to give more and more for the same money, with an ultimate result similar to the simple effect of driving the price down. As described above, this would tend to cause a reduction in quality or an increase in the risk of non-compliance elsewhere.

The fundamental fact in all this is that the purchaser may not be getting more, in spite of the higher strength or other property. The one who actually prepared the specification may have decided that a certain value was all that was required and that any increase was not usable, or simply that it provided no benefit since it was not the critical attribute or combination of attributes which contributed to increased life, performance, or other advantage. The purchaser of a valuable carpet which is said to have a life of three hundred years is really not interested in paying even 5 per cent more for one that will last a thousand years! The extra life is of no consequence to him.

Suppose that, as a result of a policy of a standardisation, it has been decided to operate with equipment of certain well-defined characteristics throughout an organisation. All efforts at setting up the facilities and communication for feeding back operational information to provide development data, are less meaningful if purchases had been made on the basis of extra properties. For then the data could not be related exactly to the characteristics specified. It might be assumed that the specification was adequate when, in fact, the purpose was being achieved by somewhat higher atrributes, etc.

If it is suspected that an increased property might be valuable, the specification should be correspondingly amended—temporarily or for a part of a purchase. Rational recording of the effects in use will then produce a justification or otherwise, when the amendment can be formalised or removed. Normally, however, no commercial advantages should be given for exceeding specified requirements—this will usually be to the disadvantage of the purchaser in the long term.

Methods of purchase not geared to lowest first cost

Most methods of purchase in use are directly concerned with getting what the *purchaser* feels is the best bargain—at that time. When, as occurs in most organisations of any size, he is not the actual user, he must be backed up with all the information which he may need in order to ensure that the *user* gets the best bargain. The provision of a specification, or the use of some such systems, involving the user, as an Approval System (discussed later), are good means of giving this support. The involvement of the purchaser in the feed of information between the user and the supplier is another example, although this method is not always practicable nor, in some case, desirable. The commitment of most methods of purchase to first cost only, with no consideration of performance, life, etc, is far too common although not justified except against strictly defined requirements.

Possible effect of arrangements for budgetary control

It might be considered that this situation arises as a result of the methods of provision of money for the purchases. Requisitions or applications for the purchase of equipment or commodities are usually in the form of quotations of first price together with justifications, and it is often required that more than one alternative or quotation is submitted. Ultimate agreement is based on these simple facts, with the result that it is decided to permit the purchase of A at £1000 rather than B at £1200, regardless of the eventual result that A lasts three years whereas B might have lasted five years. The systems of application for finance are often such that actual authorisation for spending need only be sought for an initial purchase and not for subsequent possibly higher costs of spares, maintenance, etc. It is then convenient—that is, least nuisance—to seek the purchase of lowest first cost.

The magnitude and effect of "cost of ownership"

At the Fourth Annual American Reliability and Maintenance Conference held in Los Angeles at the end of July 1965, a Government Agency speaker referred to a recent Department of Defence investigation into the "cost of ownership" of its purchased equipment. This cost included the cost of purchase or acquisition—that is, first cost—the costs of running or using, the cost of maintenance, spares, replacement, and so on, all totalled during the useful life of the equipment. It was found to vary in the range from three to twenty times the cost of acquisition. From this investigation many things followed immediately:

1   Purchasing on the basis of minimum cost of ownership would be an ideal solution where practicable.
2   The first price, which tends to be of low significance compared with the cost of ownership, should be examined in the light of whether a supplier can give greater overall economy with a higher reliability. Since a higher price would be involved, this must be supported by the supplier with meaningful guarantees for his claims.
3   Reliability considerations should be based on periodical reviews of maintenance practice and schedules, and the effect of their frequency on minimising the cost of ownership.

Purchasers can initiate exercises to determine the cost of ownership. The rate of usage of certain components or replacements can be recorded for the benefit of both user and supplier. This, incidentally, promotes development in the form of the steps which may then be

141

taken to reduce those rates which are unnecessarily high. Suppliers should be encouraged to provide necessary maintenance data, as in motor-car handbooks. Operators can record running costs in the form of power or materials used, fuel oil, etc, and, of course, ultimate useful life. Even without a great deal of this data, the submission of a request to purchase equipment should compare not only first costs but also probable costs of ownership in as much detail as possible at the time. In this way, the purchaser is working for the benefit of the user. Those responsible for determining the allocation of finances for purchase are made aware of the best value.

On the other hand, since the cost of ownership may be several times the first cost, the presentation should normally seek provision of money for first cost only, with the evidence of cheaper overall costs as support. It would be unwise to seek the total cost in one budget. Where it might be a profitable pursuit, thought should be given by the purchaser to the possibility of buying, for example, a machine and any necessary spares, for so many years for a single sum of money. In this way the manufacturer of better equipment is given a bonus (by requiring less attention and spares), while the manufacturer of inferior equipment would suffer a corresponding penalty.

Purchase by life. Where the commodity has a value largely determined by its longevity in the working circumstances, and where the other criteria of cost of ownership (spares, running costs, and so on) are not relevant or of low significance, consideration should be given to purchasing on a life basis. This can only be done when some idea of the value of life is known and is, therefore, rarely possible except where a commodity is in continuous purchase and suitable operational monitoring is proceeding. In the case of a linear loss of life (*see page 107*) it may be possible to provide some reasonably accurate values of life by means of accelerated life tests. Otherwise, it may be possible for a supplier to make a claim (which can be substantiated later) and support it with some sort of guaranteed minimum life.

If it were possible to purchase on the basis of life, this could be done by means of the ratio price per unit life discussed earlier. The prices proposed by the supplier would be adjusted by information on life and, if necessary, compared with similar data from competitors and an index proportional to the price per unit life used.

An example is in the application of paint for the protection of structures against the weather. Samples of metal, a few inches square, can be treated with different paints, placed in a position exposed to sun, wind, and rain, and examined every few months. In this way, cheap even for large numbers of samples, a view of price per unit of life can be obtained. The tests should continue even after purchasing has taken place, since information accumulated increases the accuracy of judgement and permits the checking of consistency.

This case is interesting not only for the direct material savings, but also for the even greater economies achieved by the reduction in labour required to apply the paint—which is usually more expensive.

The advantages of purchasing in this way are to both sides. Clearly, the user benefits for he is paying for usage. But the supplier also benefits. With virtually all purchases, the supplier is usually inhibited from charging more for his product even when it is justified. To improve it by development; to provide longer life, better performance; to provide inspection; to install test facilities, etc; all cost money. Yet there is an understandable reluctance on the part of a purchaser to pay more than is asked by another supplier for an apparently similar product. True, in the case of the dearer one, claims are being made for improvement, but the allure of the lower priced articles is strong. This is one reason for manufacturers to look at development as a non-profitable or high risk occupation and many are cynical about getting their money back, especially when selling to a large and powerful customer.

Purchasing on a life (or quality) basis, however, presents a different picture. It certainly controls development for it would be no use asking for a 10 per cent higher price when the life had only been increased by 5 per cent. But it provides the only rational way of encouraging, *and paying for*, development. Here is one way in which, by means of a price per unit life index, the improved product, though dearer, becomes competitive. Here is a way in which it becomes a worth-while investment to pay for true development.

Purchasing on the basis of usage. Of course, purchase by life can be effected even when the ultimate life is not known, by paying at intervals of use instead of a single original sum. This is equivalent to buying a service instead of a thing. Examples in which this type of arrangement exists have been payments by a large transport organisation to a tyre manufacturer on a mileage basis. In exchange for keeping all vehicles properly "shod" at all times, there is a periodical payment per numbers of thousands of miles travelled. Similarly, in a tunnelling contract, the engineers could buy drilling rather than drills. They would pay the supplier for drills and drillers or on the basis of a yardage tunnelled. Sometimes, the payments are linear—that is, uniform throughout—in other cases, the price per unit service falls successively to a minimum value.

This method of purchase, where possible and practicable in the light of all the circumstances, is mutually beneficial to purchaser and user, as with all cases of purchase *other* than by first cost alone. The user pays to achieve his actual purpose and the supplier has a vested interest in the increased reliability or life of his equipment. Breakdowns, loss of life, or other sources of unreliability are costly to both.

Approval of manufacturer by vendor rating

"Vendor rating" is an arbitrary system of grading suppliers. The criteria by which this is done are those in which the purchaser is interested, namely quality, cost, and delivery. The order of importance of these may, of course, vary from one purchase to another, but the rating provides a means of estimating the relative advantages to be expected by purchasing from one, rather than from another supplier.

Quality achievement in both level and consistency of supply is recorded as a result of examination of the inspection records, either at the factory or of the user's own inspection system. These measure the supplier's "efficiency" in complying with requirements as well as degree of satisfaction with his rectification or replacement procedures. Delivery performance and cost are obtained from purchasing records, which enable a judgement to be made as to the probability of receiving the goods on time, etc.

Details of various possible vendor rating formalities, which should be tailor-made for particular purposes and which, at best, are based on arbitrary scales of measurement or simply grades *A*, *B*, or *C*, are available from many sources. [For example, *A Guide to Supplier's Quality Assurance*, Institution of Production Engineers.] They are often bound up with the first—that is, quality—requirement and appear sometimes in quality assurance procedures. It is sometimes better to devise one's own system, not a difficult task.

A word of caution must be uttered here. It is an absurdity to upset a "status quo" merely because of the introduction of such a system as manufacturer approval. When suppliers have been proceeding satis- factorily for some considerable time before the existence of a system,

144

it would be the height of folly to stop them until approval had been gained. The correct attitude in such a case, is to seek reasons for not approving—that is, assume approval unless otherwise demonstrated with factual evidence available to the supplier. In this way the supply of satisfactory goods can go on during the introduction of the system and the acquisition of approval.

Requirement for Q C systems

When the purchaser is a member of a large organisation, the power of the purchaser being high, there is a tendency for principles and equities to give ground. This is particularly true of those organisations which are so large that they constitute virtually whole markets in themselves. Great care has to be exercised in the methods of purchase which provide maximum benefit to both user and supplier and which do not militate unfairly against particular suppliers. For instance, requirements for quality control systems and personnel as a prerequisite to purchase, can easily operate unfairly against the small supplier and to the advantage of the big supplier who can afford to install these facilities. It must always be borne in mind that successful purchasing results in the provision of good products, not good controls; that the controls are only the means and not the end, and that the supply of good and consistent quality is itself justification for whatever methods (or even lack of methods) are in use. For this reason, wherever there are formalised requirements or documentation covering the conditions of supply in terms of quality, it is particularly necessary to ensure that no stipulations whatever have any over-riding effect on the ultimate requirement of the appropriate supplies.

Approval of product

Steps in an approval system. Although it is satifactory to note that the position is changing, purchasing has usually to be effected without a specification. Sometimes there is a specification of certain features only; in other cases a specification may be in preparation and awaiting experience of use. It is therefore necessary to make other provisions for purchase, and one of these is the application of an Approval System.

This is a means of ensuring that certain minimum requirements, either in one or more characteristics or in consistency, are maintained. It is applied rather to the products than to the suppliers responsible for them and is different from the approval of suppliers in terms of, for example, rating, which has more widespread implications including delivery performance, etc.

An Approval System is a formalised set of procedures identical for all products to which it is applied. It must be communicated to would-be suppliers in formal and accurate terms so that they are clear as to the necessary steps involved. There are:

1   The potential supplier submits a sample for examination and testing. The degree of testing depends very much on the circumstances and the nature of the product or commodity. It may comprise straightforward laboratory testing or operational testing, or both. If a part specification is involved, the first type of testing is usually necessary to determine compliance in at least that respect. Whatever the procedure, however, it is clearly defined by the user to the supplier so that the latter can make his own tests before the submission. It is wasteful to both sides if a sample fails an elementary test. Therefore, it is in the supplier's own interests to take all steps to ensure that what he submits is likely to be acceptable and not cause a (possibly irritating) waste of time and resources. The user's interests are similarly safeguarded by not testing unsatisfactory samples during a time when he could be using his facilities to test good ones. The necessary observation and recordings must be made by the user whatever the type of testing involved and the actual results, together with any analysis or comment, are given to the supplier. These will help in the case of any further submissions, or in subsequent production, or even in development work.

If the results are deemed to be satisfactory, a Provisional Approval is recommended on technical grounds by the testing personnel to the purchaser.

2   Having had satisfactory submission, the purchaser makes any necessary commercial investigations into the standing of the prospective supplier as to his ability to supply. If satisfied by these inquiries, he then asks for a "specification" *rigorously fixing* the details of the sample submitted. This may only be a list of the characteristics and should not include the test requirement or any other features not necessary to "freeze" the quality of the sample unambiguously. This document is

lodged with the purchaser, at high level (in confidence if the situation so demands), with the object of ensuring that there is recorded all detail necessary to provide an exact replica of what was tested. When this has been done, the purchaser then awards the recommended Provisional Approval to the manufacturer, formalising it by means of an identification, such as a number, which is related to that particular design and materials. The Provisional Approval Number is given with the clear understanding, also recorded for both parties, that no modification can be made to that specification except with the agreement of the actual *user*. Any request is made through the purchaser, who might decide to change the PAN if a further recommendation is made.

3   The allotting of a PAN permits (but does not necessarily guarantee) purchase. What has been achieved so far is a demonstration that the manufacturer or supplier is *capable* of making the approved articles as a single prototype. If it is agreed to purchase, this is usually in moderate quantities at first. The purchaser takes whatever steps are necessary to check that his supplies are consistent with the original sample and its test results. This he may do by assuring himself of the means of control of quality of the supplier and by the imposition of his own inspection at frequencies determined by necessity.

4   After a suitable time, one article is selected at random direct from production by the purchaser or his representative and removed for submission to the same tests or test procedures as were applied to the original sample. If the results are satisfactory, it has now been reasonably demonstrated that the supplier is capable of maintaining the required quality in production, at that rate, and under those particular conditions of process and control of quality.

5   As a result of this, the Provisional Approval is converted to a full Approval by the purchaser, on the recommendation of the testing or using authority. Purchasing can now proceed normally.

6   During production, the control of quality must remain as effective as before. The purchaser has to be assured of this by making his own checks or inspection, whose frequency is greater or less according to his findings. He can delegate the full responsibility for quality to the supplier, but never cede his own rights of ultimate determination that he "gets what he

pays for." In particular, he must watch out for changes in the production processes, in the actual equipment of production, in the rate of production, and in the various personnel responsible. Since any of these may affect the quality consistency, the formality of Approval indicates clearly that a request must be made to the purchaser to agree such a change whenever required. The agreement can be a straightforward and uncomplicated assent or might involve reapproval in some form—both, however, necessitating technical advice.

7   All requests for submission to the Approval System must be channelled properly. It would create chaos if they were made to different people, the purchaser or the user (if they are different). Since the examinations are technical it is necessary that a technical man or an actual user be given the formal responsibility to conduct all the arrangements, correspondence, tests, and programmes appropriate to the whole of the operations. He also evaluates test results and makes any necessary recommendations to his purchasing colleague. The latter is kept aware of the fact of the submission and is ultimately responsible for the actual award of Approval. This is necessary because it is usual for the Approval, as with a specification, to be part of any contractual arrangement.

This type of focusing is helpful both to the user and to the supplier. It creates an orderly flow of information and provides the right atmosphere for improvement of quality and for development generally. It is essential to the success of Approval Systems.

Finally, a word about approval with a small *a*. This should be differentiated from Approval above, which is a particular series of formalities. Unless the user has a design unit capable of handling the whole of the design and testing of everything he purchases (or, which is is purchased for him), it is usually unwise for him to accede to a request for the "approval" of anything. In so doing, he automatically accepts some of the responsibility for the design, construction, materials, methods, etc. This responsibility is that of the supplier alone (except in the case of the user supplying a specification, which involves no approval).

When faced with such a request from a supplier, therefore, a suitable procedure would be to ask the latter to state a number of claims for what he wishes to sell. These should be in a form capable of substantiation by measurement, test, or operation. After an adequate period of experience, these claims can then be "agreed" as necessary by the user, who should on no account commit himself by the use of terms including the word "approve."

Technical considerations for purchasing

In an organisation in which the purchasing is performed by personnel other than the actual users, they are often confronted with technical problems. These are problems to which only the user or his technical colleagues can provide answers. There must therefore be a constant and free communication between the two parties. Sometimes the purchaser tries to save his colleagues trouble by making decisions himself—for example, about the purchase of quality—which have technical implications. On other occasions, he may be unaware of the technical implications of their gravity. The only remedy for this situation is for each party to have a working knowledge of the other's responsibilities to the extent that they recognise a position requiring advice. Since it is the purchaser who is in direct contact with the supplier, it is doubly important that he is aware of technical implications, though only in a non-professional general way so that he can ask the necessary questions of the user of supplier. Some of the problems which arise are described below.

Relation of cost of intrinsic Q and R to that of the system. In purchasing a component, machine, or any commodity which is to be part of a system, the quality and reliability required must also be related to the system or method of use. Since quality and reliability cost money, the questions to be asked are whether the values sought have been arrived at intrinsically, or in relation to the overall system or usage, and whether the cost of these values is an important part of the total cost or not. As has been described elsewhere, the overall reliability of a system is the product of all the units in series. It would therefore be of little value, if the rest of the system is satisfactory at a reliability of 60 per cent, for one to spend a great deal of extra money in order to raise one part of the system from 90 to 95 per cent. Thus, as far as the purchaser is concerned, the relation of cost to the reliability of an individual item is a matter which cannot be isolated from the reliability of the whole system of which the item may be a small part. For this reason, a

149

purchaser must (tactfully) draw attention to requirements of high reliability where these involve substantial additional costs, and ensure that the user has considered these in the light of the system.

One aspect of purchasing by life in which relation to system is of particular importance, is the consideration of which life and which cost are the relevant factors, that of the particular purchase or that of the system of which it is a part. To illustrate this, let us assume that the article to be purchased is critical to a system but costs only one-tenth of the total. If by trebling the price, the life of the system is extended by 50 per cent, then effectively an increase in system life of one-and-a-half times is gained by an outlay only 20 per cent more. The correct examination therefore concerns itself with the cost of the whole system and the life of the whole system. This is particularly the case with "insurance" items such as safety devices, and with units which can be considered as connecting links in one form or another. The fact that such a link may cost ten times as much to double *its* life might appear to a purchaser to be a bad bargain. If the overall consideration is looked at, it may be seen that the whole system, costing a thousand times more than the link, can be operated with a breakdown or outage frequency reduced to half. (Attention has also to be paid to change in the repair time, of course.) Thus, it is the duty of a purchaser to seek out information as to the consequences of this type of purchase, before making a decision based on too narrow a view. He must ensure that the right cost is related to the right life and not confine himself to looking at one small part of a system.

Cost of too high levels of quality and reliability

Although it is also strictly a technical consideration, the level of quality may concern a purchaser in the case of general supplies. It is then necessary for him to learn something about the method of use to which such commodities may be put. For example, if, in the purchase of nuts and bolts, it were known that these were to be used in the assembly of important machines, it might be assumed that the quality requirement would be high. In that case, the manufacturer, informed that every single nut and bolt had to be compliant with the requirement, would apply a possibly expensive process of control with corresponding effects on the price. On making inquiries into the method of use, however, it is found that the fitter picked the nuts and bolts out of a bin, throwing away the odd one which appeared to be defective. In this case, it pays to purchase at a lower price than that which would be charged for the certainty that every nut and bolt complied. Some sampling inspection scheme less comprehensive can give best value for money and still achieve what is required.

Purchaser's rights to quality. On the other hand, unless the mutually agreed arrangements were in the form of an acceptance of, say, at least 95 per cent good products, the purchaser is entitled to get 100 per cent good. The manufacturer has to consider whether the *possible* requirements of a replacement of a few per cent of the goods found to be defective is a cheaper and more convenient procedure than the installation of a more expensive control system. This arrangement should be known to both parties and the reasons made clear and acceptable. When it is a good bargain for the purchaser, and not inconvenient to the user himself, he may wish to look at his documentation for control requirements. If necessary, he should modify these parts calling for rigorous procedures guaranteeing the certainty of 100 per cent good articles, if by so doing he is providing for the user's purpose in a perfectly reasonable manner, and yet enjoying a better bargain. Needless to say, this cannot be done without full consultation with the user himself, and the understanding of the supplier that defectives will still have to be replaced.

So far, we have looked at the problem of purchasing a number of things. What about the purchase of only one? Woe betide the supplier who, in dealing with a subsequent complaint from a customer to whom one unit or equipment was sold, tries to explain away the customer's dissatisfaction in probability terms. "You may be interested to know, madam, that your washing machine is the only one in 2000 which we have sold which has so far failed."

This is, of course, absolutely no comfort for the customer; her money was good and she has a right to expect what she paid for and what was claimed. It may well be that the supplier shows that he has taken all reasonable steps to ensure reliability of the order of 0.9995 and that only about one defective in 2000 could be expected, but probabilities and statistics are for reliability experts and controls staff—never for customers.

Purchasing in cases of failure of quality

As has been discussed previously (*see pages 69–74*) the purchaser may be faced with a departure from quality. Of the three cases mentioned, the first, which referred to the requirements for exemption, does not concern him except indirectly. He has, of course, to do all he can to optimise his purchasing, and any internal requests which result in having to make some special arrangements adversely affect his performance. Nevertheless, it is not for him to interfere with what is normally purely a technical matter.

In the case of the other two, manufacturing departures are involved and requests for a manufacturing permit or a concession must come directly to the purchasing office, as being in contravention of the contract. Decisions, however, usually require technical assent and it is necessary for him to check that all marginal non-compliances are acceptable to the user, as merely a matter of convenience. Where the user declines to accept, the purchaser has no overriding powers.

In cases of a mandatory or statutory requirement for safety, the law has taken all powers out of a purchaser's hands and non-compliance is unacceptable.

Appendix One

Typical Complaints Code

Delivery

1   *Time element.*

Promise broken once/more times.
Packing delay.
Delivery schedules ignored.
Stock not held as required.
Time exceeded causing cancellation.
Time excessive, thus losing order.

2   *Material element.*

Wrong goods sent.
Wrong size sent.
Wrong quantities sent (including duplication, over-delivery).
Wrong dimensions sent.

Quality

1   *Materials.*

Wrong material.
Foreign matter, dirt, etc.

2   *Manufacture.*

Bad manufacture.
Wrong assembly.
Poor finish.

3 *Control.*

Inconsistency (lack of uniformity of quality).
Non-compliance with specification.
Faulty inspection.

4 *Design.*

Unsuitable for purpose, through compliant with specification—
that is, specification inadequate, abuse, or overload.

Customer orientation

1 *Internal.*

Clerical errors (wrong addresses, coding, loss of correspondence,
or orders).

2 *Time element.*

Delay in quoting.
Interdepartmental delays.
Delay in handling paper, or issuing credits.
Delay in replying to customer or representative (letter or phone).
Failure to reply to customer or representative (letter or phone).

3 *External errors.*

Customer's inspection or wrong information.
Customer's requests wrongly stated by him in error.
Customer's requests wrongly stated by him by lack of know-
ledge.
Inadequate attention to customer's requests.
Lack of interest in him—by person, letter, or phone.

4 *Samples.*

Samples not available.
Inappropriate charges for samples.

Miscellaneous Complaints

Appendix Two

Guide to the Preparation of Specifications (Extract)

Comprehensive list of items which may be required in a specification

1 *Title of specification*. Care should be exercised when choosing a title for a specification so that no ambiguity can arise. The wording chosen should preferably be capable of fitting into indexing or classification schemes and be capable of easy and unambiguous translation into other languages. In addition, the appropriate classification index, such as the Universal Decimal Classification, should be included. Consideration should be given to the numbering and dating of the specification so that there is no confusion with previous or subsequent issues. The title may indicate whether the specification is written primarily from the using, designing, manufacturing, or selling point of view.

2 *List of contents*.

3 *Foreword*.

3.1 *History and background information.* The Foreword should state, as appropriate, any background information, the reason why the specification has been written, the authority for its preparation, and the name of the issuing authority. Any special features of the specification should be mentioned, such as limitations to which it is desired to call attention and comments on particular aspects. In the revision of a previous specification, it is often useful to give a general indication of the reasons for the revision, and the principal changes made.

The Foreword is the appropriate place for any general observations of a non-mandatory nature, and for the mention of standards in the same series or otherwise related—but not to the standards to which references are required for working to the specification. (*See 8 below.*)

It should be noted that the Foreword does not form part of the specification and should not be used to lay down mandatory requirements, all of which should be included in the specification clauses.

4 *Scope of the specification.*

4.1 *The extent and limitations of the subject matter to be covered in the specification. A brief description of item/material covered. Range of sizes, ratings, compositions, grades, etc. Code numbers or other designations for ordering purposes.*

If the specification is limited to certain features only—for example, workmanship and dimensions—this should be stated. In some instances it may be necessary, where it is not otherwise obvious, to draw attention to excluded features.

5 *The role of the equipment or material.* Information in this clause may be valuable to the designer in interpreting the user's requirements, to the manufacturer in interpreting the designer's requirements, etc. It may be appropriate in some specifications to include this under 4.

6 *Definitions.* Attention is drawn to the fact that authoritative information on terminology, symbols, abbreviations, and measuring systems exists in British Standards and reference should be made to these wherever possible.

6.1 *Terminology.* In order to avoid possible misunderstanding of the meanings of terms used in the specification it is often necessary to define the terms. These include the precise meanings to be applied to normal English words, such as "should," "shall," "inspect," "examine," as well as technical terms, if necessary citing a particular dictionary, reference book, or standard glossary. Where appropriate, reference to this clause may be made in later clauses of the specification.

6.2 *Symbols and abbreviations.* Precise meaning of any symbols and abbreviations used should be given.

6.3 *Measuring systems.* Besides laying down the units of measurement used in the specification, for example, metric (SI units) or inch, it may be necessary to refer to other conventions such as first or third angle projections in drawings, etc.

6.4 *Language.* Where the specification is the concern of different countries it may be necessary to specify the language of the document or related documents to which reference is made.

7 *Relevant authorities to be consulted.* Attention should be drawn to any other authorities which may need to be consulted in relation to the equipment or material. For example, in the case of a manufacturing specification it may be necessary to obtain the clearance of a safety officer before proceeding with a particular process. A selling specification may mention the need for a prospective user to consult health authorities, factory inspectors, etc.

8 *Related documents and references.*

8.1 *Reference to user/design/manufacturing specification.*

8.2 *Statutory regulations or other legal conditions.*

8.3 *British Standards and Codes of Practice.*

8.4 *National standards of other countries or international standards or regulations.*

8.5 *Standards issued by other bodies—for example, nationalised industries, trade associations.*

8.6 *Other regulations/documents applicable.* The extent of the applicability of related documents and references should be made clear.

9 *Conditions in which the item or material is to be installed, used, manufactured, or stored.*

9.1 *Environmental features including for example:*

temperature;	*pressure;*	*humidity;*	*altitude;*	*shock;*
vibration;	*terrain;*	*atmosphere;*	*noise;*	*dust;*
infestation;	*radiation;*	*fluid;*	*chemicals;*	*electrical interference*

A number of features of environment are included as examples; these could be extended indefinitely. It is important to note that many items work in a combination of parameters—for example, high humidity and high temperature—and it is important to state these as a combination so that allowance can be made. It is possible that in some cases the effect of combined parameters could be unexpected from the individual effects. The duration of exposure to environment is important as also is any cycle of environmental conditions.

9.2 *Relations to associated equipment—for example, compatibility with other items in an assembly, influence on environment.*

9.3 *Conditions of use, power requirements, supply services.* An indication should be given of the conditions and the personnel operating the equipment, as it may be necessary for the supplier to make special provisions for operation by unskilled labour, or even for a certain amount of abuse. This clause is usually appropriate for the user-to-designer or designer-to-manufacturer type of specification.

9.4 *Servicing requirements including access.* Difficulties should be stated regarding accessibility for servicing or other limitations which might affect the design of the product.

10 *Characteristics.*

10.1 *Design, samples, drawings, models, preliminary tests, or investigations.* The user may only be able to indicate his requirements in a very general way, i.e. by stating purpose or function. A designer will give adequate instructions for a design which he considers will embody the user's requirements. The manufacturing specification meets these requirements in terms of the final product. Consultation and agreement are necessary at all stages.

10.2 *Properties—for example, strength, dimensions, weight, safety, degree of purity, taste, etc—with tolerances where appropriate.* It may be necessary to indicate those properties which are critical and those which are not critical.

10.3 *Interchangeability (functional, dimensional).*

10.4 *Materials and their properties (including permissible variability), approved or excluded materials, effect of repair.* Alternative materials should be included where possible; variability refers to acceptable tolerances on supplies of raw materials, etc. It may be necessary to specify particular materials with a view to ease of repair, subsequent processing, etc.

10.5 *Requirements for a manufacturing process.* A manufacturing process—for example, heat treatment or forging—should be specified only when it is critical to design considerations. In other cases, the specification of the particular processes should be avoided as possibly stultifying new developments.

10.6 *Appearance, texture, finish, including colour, protection, etc.*

10.7 *Identification marks, operating symbols on controls, weight of items, safety indications, etc.*

10.8 *Method of marking.* The following details are typical:

(*a*)   The name, trademark, or other means of identifying the manufacturer.

(*b*)   The date of manufacture, or batch and, where possible, identification to machine or operator.

(*c*)   The nominal size, rating, or other relevant particulars of any coding of the materials.

(*d*)   The reference number of the specification to which the product is supplied.

The position of such marks and their method of application should also be detailed.

11 Performance.

11.1 *Performance under specified conditions.* The user should describe in his specification the stipulated requirements. Some may not be possible or economic. The designer may, therefore, wish to make some adjusting statements in accordance with the practicability of the design. A selling specification may make a claim for performance which may be in excess of user's requirements. Such claims should be related to tests, guarantees and/or certification schemes.

11.2 *Test methods and equipment for assessing performance: where, how, and by whom carried out; reference to correlation with behaviour in operation.* It is important for specifications where applicable to set out as clearly as possible types of test, test methods, and procedures. In certain cases where the commissioning and acceptance of major complexes are concerned, it may be impracticable to complete tests other than when the assembly is installed; in this instance it is important that agreement is reached by all parties concerned as to where, how, and by whom the tests are carried out. Where possible, the methods and procedures used should be in accordance with nationally recognised standard methods. [*See*, for example, the *British Standards Yearbook*.] In cases where it is not possible to reproduce conditions of operation, it may be necessary to consider performance in comparative terms and reference to correlation between test results and operational use should be made.

11.3 *Criteria for passing tests, including accuracy of results and interpretation of results.* The exact criteria by which the material or item is deemed to pass the tests should be set out. It may be necessary to employ different criteria in the case of numbers of items or bulk quantity. In certain cases a percentage of failures to pass the tests, or a tolerance on performance, may be acceptable.

11.4 *Acceptance conditions.* Acceptance conditions may be stated in terms of full compliance with the requirements of the above clauses. On the other hand, certain modifying or additional statements may be needed.

11.5 *Certification and/or reporting.* Details should be given of any reports, test schedules, or certificates required.

12 *Life*.

12.1 *Period of useful life.* The period of useful life is that period over which the performance does not drop below a tolerable level, having regard to reliability. It should be stipulated by the user or designer and may be claimed by the seller. The period of useful life is dependent on proper servicing and maintenance as would be laid down under Clause 16, and proper overhaul, as defined in 12.2.

12.2 *Life between overhauls.* "Overhaul" is used in the context of a significant operation rather than routine servicing, but what exactly is involved should be clearly defined. It may be stipulated by the user and designer in relation to the operating process and should be claimed or advised by the seller.

12.3 *Total life.* Total life is the period over which *some* performance can be obtained; it usually exceeds the useful life of a product by a period in which it is accepted that performance levels may be falling. Where decline in performance is not a gradual process, the total life may, in effect, be the same as the useful life.

12.4 *Test methods and equipment for assessing life.*

12.5 *Criteria including accuracy and interpretation of results of tests.*

12.6 *Acceptance conditions.*

12.7 *Certification and/or reporting.*

13 *Reliability.*

13.1 *Reliability under stipulated conditions.* Reliability under stipulated conditions may be expressed in many different ways—for example, a probability of performing as required under specified conditions for a specified time or number of cycles, or an acceptable maximum failure rate. The reliability should be specified by the user or designer and where it is claimed by the seller, the bases of the claims should be indicated.

13.2 *Control procedures, test methods and equipment for assessing reliability, bases for claims.* These may be stipulated by the user and designer and should be quoted as a basis for any claims made in a selling specification.

13.3 *Criteria including accuracy and interpretation of results of tests, confidence levels.*

13.4 *Acceptance conditions.*

13.5 *Certification and/or reporting.* Details should be given of any reports, test schedules, or certificates required. It may also be necessary to refer here to any arrangements for feed-back of information to the manufacturer of operational experience or data obtained by the user.

14 *Control of quality; checking for compliance with specification.*

Note: The declaration of quality is incorporated in Clauses 10 to 13.

This is one of the most important sections of the specification. Any process of control of quality which is considered necessary to maintain the uniformity of quality of the product should be stipulated. In particular, sampling procedure and interpretation should be introduced where appropriate. Any declaration of quality made by the seller should be related to the detailed methods of control of quality set out in the specification clauses.

14.1 *Method of checking compliance.*

14.2 *Production tests on raw materials, components, sub-assemblies, and assemblies; records to be kept by the manufacturer.*

14.3 *Assurance of compliance—for example, by supplier's certificates or independent certification schemes.*

14.4 *Inspection facilities required by the user/designer or offered by the manufacturer/supplier.*

14.5 *Instructions regarding reject material or items.*

14.6 *Instructions in regard to modifications of process.* Where, for example, a worn-out machine is replaced or a process is removed from one site to another the user may wish to re-establish, by some agreed means, the continued compliance with the specification.

14.7 *Applicability of requirements of* 14.1 *to* 14.6 *to sub-contractors, etc.*

14.8 *Acceptance conditions.*

15 *Packaging and protection.*

15.1 *Specification of packaging, including any special conditions in transit.* Reference may be made to tests required for the package, the British Standard Packaging Code and other relevant packaging specifications.

15.2 *Conditions in which required/supplied.* Certain relevant details may be required of the condition of the article as supplied—for example, protected, refrigerated, lubricant-free—which are not covered under physical characteristics.

15.3 *Period of storage.*

15.4 *Marking of packaging.* Any special marks or other coding details required on the packaging in addition to those marked on the component or material itself (*see* 10.8) should be stipulated.

16 *Information from the supplier to the user.* This section deals with the information which the user may ask to be given by the supplier, or alternatively, information which, without any specific requests for it, the supplier will give to the user. It is important that information on maintenance frequency and any limitations should be clearly set out by the supplier as this will have a bearing on the performance, reliability, and life to be expected from the product.

162

16.1 *Instructions for storage, taking into use, advice on installation, operation, and maintenance.*

16.2 *Service facilities and access, lubricants to be used, fuels, replacement parts, etc.*

16.3 *Maintenance details, frequency, and limitations.*

16.4 *Relevant literature—for example, handbooks of operations, spare parts manuals, codes of practice.*

17 *After sales service.*

17.1 *Facilities available or required.*

17.2 *Guarantees and warranties.*

17.3 *Complaints and compensation procedure.* Guarantees and warranties, complaints procedures, etc, are not normally detailed in a specification, but the requirement to supply information on these may be specified. The facilities available for after sales service may form a large feature of a selling specification.

Index

ACCELERATED LIFE 106–8
Approval of manufacturer by vendor rating 144–5
Approval systems 140, 145–9
provisional approval and provisional approved numbers (PAN) 146–7
Association Française de Normalisation 59
Automation 40–1

BARLOW, RICHARD E 116
Battersby, A 46
Beadon, Commander J A 9
British Productivity Council xiii
British Standards Institution (BSI) 59
PD 6112 (*Guide to the Preparation of Specifications*) 63
Budgetary control and purchase 140–1

CLEAVER, P C 9
Company objectives 26–8
Complaints:
code 19–20, 153–4
procedure for handling 90–1
Concessions 73–4
Control of quality:
internal organisation 23–5
linkage with customers 21–3
overall 20–5
see also Quality Control
'Cost of ownership' of purchased equipment 141–3
purchase by life 142–3
Coutinho, John de S 132
Customers:
advice to 18–19
linkage with 21–3
requirements 13–14

DEFECTS:
in manufacture 129
isolation and elimination 53–7
overall severity 55
relative severity 54–6
source 55–6
tolerable level 53–4
vital few 56–7
Delegated information 88
Delivery 3
Departmental manager's responsibilities 30
Design:
definitions 126–7
embodiment of requirements 14
'factors of safety' 128
inadequacy 126–9
margin for variation in quality 128
operating conditions beyond assumptions 129–30
quality of design 16
wider requirements 127
Destructive testing 110–12
welding 112
Deutscher Normenausschuss 59
Development:
and standardisation 98–102
improvement and innovation 94–114
increase in reliability 115–32

EUROPEAN ORGANISATION FOR QUALITY CONTROL 63
Evaluation, testing for 117–18

FACTORY INSPECTION 77–84
inspector's functions 77–9
organisation 82–4

165

FACTORY INSPECTION—*continued*
reduction of manufacturing risks 80
variation and rejection 80–2
Fatigue testing 112–13
interpretation of tests 113
Fleet Air Arm, reliability problems 9

GUARANTEES 17
limitations 5–6
*Guide to Supplier's Quality Assurance,
A* (Institution of Production
Engineers) 144
Guide to the Preparation of Specifications 63–4

HUMAN CONTRIBUTION TO QUALITY
26–42
automation 40–1
checklist for good organisation
28
company objectives and background
to Q and R activities 26–8
industrial motivations 38–40
middle management responsibility
28–9
physical characteristics of people
36–8
shop floor management 30–5
workers and standards 41–2

IMPROVEMENT AND INNOVATION:
and development 94–6
development and standardisation
98–102
middle management and development
policy 96–8
specification test equipment
109–14
types of testing 102–9
Increase in reliability 115–32
*Increasing the Efficiency of Development
Testing* (Pratt and Whitney
Aircraft Corporation) 124
Increasing the proportion of good
quality 43–57
isolation and elimination of defects
53–7
monitoring performance 41, 46–53
product examination 43–6
Industrial motivations 38–40
criteria of success 39

Information feed from operations to
manufacturer 19–20
checklist 20
complaints code 19–20, 153–4
Inspection and inspection departments
18, 24
checking after receipt 85–6
delegated inspection 88
factors affecting standards 89–90
factory inspection 77–84
inspection at manufacture 86–7
inspection by users 84–93
personal qualities of inspectors 93
procedure for handling complaints
90–1
programme of visits 92
resident inspection 87–8
role in ensuring quality 77–93
storekeeper's duties 85
'vetting' of manufacturers 88–9
Institution of Production Engineers
144
International Organisation for Standardisation (ISO) 59, 63

LARGE ORGANISATIONS:
and inspection 84
special effects of standardisation
65–6
Life, testing for 105–8, 112
accelerated life 106–8
definitions of aspects of "life" 106
life patterns 106
linear life 107

MACHINE MANAGEMENT 33–4
Man management 30–3
efficient use of men 31–3
operator training 31–2
Manufacturers:
approval by vendor rating 144–5
concessions 73–4
departure from specification
69–74
exemptions 70–1
manufacturing permits 71–3
'vetting' of 88–9
Manufacturing risks, reduction of 80
Market orientation 13
Mass flow movement 46–7
Material, management of 35

Mathematical Theory of Reliability (Barlow) 116
Measurement of reliability 117–18
Middle management:
  and development policy 96–8
  responsibility 28–9
  teamwork 29
Minimum value, control chart 82
Monitoring performance 41, 46–56
  avoidable waste 48–9
  mass flow movement 46–7
  production performance on profit basis 49–53
  pure output measurement 46–7
  unavoidable waste 47–8

NATIONAL COAL BOARD 37
  and fire-resistant belting 9–10
  conference on reliability 9–10
National Council for Quality and Reliability xiii, 63–4
National Productivity Year (1963) xii
  Conference 8–9
Network Analysis for Planning and Scheduling (Battersby) 46
Nixon, F 36
Non-destructive testing 113–14
  ultrasonics 114

'ONE-OFF' EQUIPMENT, RELIABILITY OF 123–4
Operational data and increased reliability 124
Operational testing 102–5
  buying information from users 104–5
  influence of operating parameters 103–4
  payment 103
Operator training 31–2

PARKINSON'S LAW 23
Payment by results 41
Physcial characteristics of people 36–318
  tests and inspections 36–7
Pratt and Whitney Aircraft Corporation 124
Price per unit of quality 135–8
Probability 131–2
  concepts of 116–17
  games 131
  reliability as 115–17

Procedures and reliability 131–2
Product examination 43–6
  system and stages 46–7
Profit in Q and R 1–11
  definition of quality 1–2
  delivery 3
  economic survey of Q and R activities 8–11
  future in industry 11
  limitations of guarantees 5–6
  meaning of reliability 3–7
Profit Index (PI) 50–3
Profiting by Quality and Reliability (National Conference report) 12
Profit performance (PP) 50–3
Purchase of quality 133–52
  and budgetary control 140–1
  Approval systems 140, 145–9
  basis of usage 143–4
  cases of quality failure 151–2
  choice from range of qualities 133–35
  'cost of ownership' 141–3
  cost of too-high levels of Q and R 150–1
  methods not geared to lowest first cost 140
  price per quality unit 135–8
  purchaser's rights to quality 151
  purchasing to specification 138–40
  requirement for QC systems 145
  technical consideration 149–50
  vendor rating 144–5
Pure output measurement 46–7

Q AND R ACTIVITIES:
  background 26–8
  economic rewards 8–11
Q and R policy, basic requirements 12–25
  advice to customers 18–19
  ascertaining requirements of customer or user 13–14
  embodiment of requirements in design 14
  information feed from operations to manufacturer 19–20
  inspection 18
  manufacturer's acceptance of responsibility 16–17
  overall control of quality 20–5
  specification 14–15

Quality:
  definition 1–2
  failure of 151–2
  of conformance 16
  of design 16
  purchase of 133–52
  purchaser's rights to 151
Quality and Reliability Year (QRY)
  (1966–7) xii–xiii
  National conference 12
Quality control 18
  and purchasing 145
  departments 18, 23
  simplified chart 81
Quality managers xii

RANDOM VARIATIONS AND REJECTION
  80
Reliability:
  alternatives to 130–1
  and procedures 131–2
  as probability 115–17
  direct causes of unreliability
    126–32
  factors affecting reliability 124–6
  increase in 115–32
  meaning of 3–7
  measurement of 117–18
  of 'one-off' equipment 123–4
  of systems 118–21
  putting values to 117
  stand-by design 122–3
  testing for evaluation 117–18
  use of operational data 124
Resident inspection 87–8
Royal Air Force report on cost of
  reliability 9

SHOP FLOOR MANAGEMENT 30–5
  departmental manager's responsi-
    bility 30
  machines 33–4
  material 35
  men 30–3
Society of Automotive Engineers
  (SAE) 59
Specifications 15, 51, 58–76
  and broad standardisation 62–3
  and purchasing 138–40
  and testing 108–9
  approach to writing 60
  as instrument of policy 66–7

codes of practice 68–9
definition 58–61
departures by user and manufacturer
  69–76
difference from standardisation 58
formulation procedure 67–8
guide to preparation 63–4, 155–63
language 61–2
over-specifying 62
proving 15–16
test equipment 109–14
Standards and standardisation 41–2,
  58–76
  and development 98–102
  broad standardisation 62–3
  complex structures and cumulative
    effects 75–6
  definition 58–9
  difference from specification 58
  loss in adjustment to standard 75
  means of achieving 66–9
  objectives of standardisation 65
  reasons for standardising and not
    standardising 64–5, 75–6
  special effects in large organisa-
    tions 65–6
  standardisation practice 64–5
  standards organisations 59
Stand-by design 122–3
Statistical Quality Control xi
Storekeeper's duties 85
Systems:
  important elements in complex
    systems 121–2
  large number of components
    120–1
  reliability of 118–21

TEAMWORK 29
Testing:
  destructive 110–12
  fatigue 112–13
  for evaluation 117–18
  for life 105–8
  non-destructive 113–14
  operational 102–5
  to specification 108–9
Test rigs 105

ULTRASONICS 114
Unreliability, direct causes of
  126–32
  alternatives to reliability 130–1

defects in manufacture   129
design inadequacy   126–9
operating conditions beyond design
    assumptions   129–30
reliability and procedures   131–2
Usage, purchasing on basis of   143–4
Users:
    buying operational information from
      104–5
    departures from specification
      69–74

inspection by   84–93
requirements   13–14

VARIETIES AND REJECTION   80–2
Vendor rating   144–5

WASTE, AVOIDABLE AND UNAVOIDABLE
    47–9
Welding   112
Workers and standards   41–2
    payment by results   41